Human Resource Policies and Procedures for Nonprofit Organizations

3/27/10

Human Resource Policies and Procedures for Nonprofit Organizations

CAROL L. BARBEITO

WILEY

John Wiley & Sons, Inc.

Copyright © 2004 by John Wiley & Sons, Inc. All rights reserved.

Published by John Wiley & Sons, Inc., Hoboken, New Jersey

Published simultaneously in Canada

For general information on our other products and services, or technical support, please contact our Customer Care Department within the United States at 800-762-2974, outside the United States at 317-572-3993 or fax 317-572-4002.

Wiley also publishes its books in a variety of electronic formats. Some content that appears in print may not be available in electronic books.

For more information about Wiley products, visit our web site at *www.wiley.com*.

Library of Congress Cataloging-in-Publication Data:
Barbeito, Carol L.
    Human resources policies and procedures for nonprofit organizations / Carol L. Barbeito.
        p.   cm.
    Includes bibliographical references and index.
    ISBN 0-471-64423-4 (cloth)
    1. Nonprofit organizations—Personnel management. 2. Nonprofit organizations—Management. I. Title.
HF5549.B265 2004
658.3'01—dc22   2004009876

Printed in the United States of America

10 9 8 7 6 5 4 3 2 1

About the Author

Carol L. Barbeito, Ph.D., is president of CLB & Associates, which offers learning services in a broad range of management and leadership topics. Services include:

- Consultation
- Training
- Train the trainer
- Advanced education
- Presentations
- Applied research

Dr. Barbeito specializes in:

- Nonprofit management and leadership
- Applied research
- Planning, including long range, annual, and project
- Needs assessment
- Evaluation
- Governance and structure of organizations
- Resource development, including fund raising and earned income
- Human resource management specializing in compensation
- Capacity building for nonprofit organizations

Her company was founded in 1990. She also founded Applied Research & Development International in 1990 and was president of both organizations for 10 years. ARDI's mission was to make existing nonprofit management and leadership resources accessible and to create new knowledge through applied research.

She is the author of 22 publications including books, research reports, directories, training kits, and a video, as well as numerous articles. She has published extensively regarding nonprofit compensation and benefits since 1984. In addition, she is a frequent presenter at conferences.

From 1983 to 1989, Dr. Barbeito was executive director of Colorado's management support organization for nonprofits, Technical Assistance Center. She also founded, and was president of TAC's for profit subsidiary, Management Assistance Center, which served government, for-profit companies, and business leagues. She came to these positions following executive directorships in child care and mental health and as the regional director for a division of the State Health Department in Michigan. For many years, she was also active as a director and then president of her family's business, Rapp's Restaurant, in Arlington Heights, Illinois.

Dr. Barbeito has worked extensively in Australia for 12 years. She is affiliated, as a senior consultant, with Australia Environment International. Other international sites include Bermuda, the Czech Republic, Slovakia, Hungary, Romania, Canada, and Egypt.

Dr. Barbeito earned Bachelor of Arts and Master of Science degrees from Indiana University and a Doctor of Philosophy degree from the University of Denver. She has been active as a member and on the boards of many professional organizations and as a community volunteer.

Contact for Dr. Barbeito, CLB & Associates, 5793 Jasper Pointe Circle, Castle Rock, CO 80108 USA, 303-688-6510, 303-688-6528 FAX, carolbarbeito@msn.com.

Acknowledgment

I am grateful to my associate, Ivy Ridlen, president of Timesavers Secretarial Services, for her fine work in obtaining permissions and formatting this book for submission to John Wiley & Sons.

Contents

Preface

Nonprofit organizations provide essential functions: caring for the sick and dying, nurturing and protecting children, conservation of our history and our environment, creating beauty and inspiring our spiritual growth, and providing a voice for engaged citizens. These are just a sample of the many and varied missions that are supported by the work of paid and unpaid staff (volunteers) in the more than 2 million nonprofit organizations in the United States.

Increasing competition for resources, expanding service demands, and a growing chorus of calls for accountability result in a high-pressure situation in which nonprofit organizations must maximize their effectiveness and efficiency to be successful. The employees and volunteers who comprise the workforce for these organizations carry out their critical missions, which contribute so much to our civil society. Consequently, there is an urgent need for information and assistance to help nonprofits create an effective work environment. Recruitment, motivation, and retention of a qualified workforce require investment in development of sound human resource management policies and procedures.

Additionally, nonprofit organizations need to reduce the risk of lawsuits and claims by knowing the laws and adopting and implementing good employment practice policies. The Nonprofit Risk Management Center in its spring 1999 issue, of *Community Risk Management & Insurance*, stated that insurers report that more than 75 percent of all directors' and officers' liability claims allege wrongful employment practices.

This book provides user-friendly explanations covering a wide variety of human resource policies and procedures, with examples of related forms and supplemental information. Although the coverage of topics is extensive, it is not all-inclusive. Some polices might apply to most nonprofit organizations.

Others are more specialized; for example, there are policies about the interaction of staff and clients that will fit only certain types of direct service organizations. Each organization will need to evaluate the need for each policy and to take care to ensure that example policies are adapted to fit its situation. Further, nonprofits will need to check with their own legal counsel, especially in regard to state laws, and to be alert for the ever-evolving case law that might affect human resource management practices. Also, federal government law and regulation changes affecting employment practices may occur frequently, and employers must be alert for such changes.

The book is organized by chapters, and chapters are organized into subheadings. The Contents provides a guide to location of topics of specific interest. Rationales for policies and procedures will be discussed first, followed, when applicable, with policy examples, forms and other tools to aid in policy adoption. References are at the end of each chapter. In addition, at the end of the book you will find a number of helpful Appendices. Included is a list of action steps for attracting and retaining quality personnel, a quiz to rate yourself as a volunteer motivator, and a plan to help create a motivating environment.

We sincerely hope this book makes the job of nonprofit managers and leaders easier as they develop an effective work environment.

Carol L. Barbeito, Ph.D.

CHAPTER 1

Organization Policies

This chapter contains policies that address the organizational structure in regard to chain of command, communications, and authority.

HUMAN RESOURCE PHILOSOPHY STATEMENT

Rationale

A human resource philosophy statement specifically states the values and practices that guide the development of the organization's human resource management system. The board often works in conjunction with staff leadership to develop this statement through delegation to a human resource committee composed of its members and sometimes other volunteers. The executive director then can conduct activities related to the human resource function of the nonprofit so actions are in concert with philosophy.

Expressed within the philosophy are strategies that will differ among organizations. In the example provided by the Applied Research & Development International (ARDI), the company stresses that it is seeking to hire highly motivated individuals who demonstrate exceptional potential for success. This strategy resulted from the realization that ARDI could not afford to pay at the top of the competitive scale for more seasoned professionals for all positions, but it desired and needed to obtain quality performance from its employees. It could offer an attractive professional growth opportunity for employees who were in the early stages of their careers and were highly motivated to establish a track record. ARDI was funded largely through "soft money" project grants, and employees sometimes were hired for the period of time covered by a specific grant. The philosophy acknowledges that turnover may occur due to this funding pattern and avoids negative interpretation of such staff changes that might otherwise raise executive performance concerns.

Each organization needs to examine the values and strategies that fit its situation and reflect them in the human resource policy statement. Creation of such statement takes time from a dedicated group of board members and may require assistance from a human resource specialist if the board does not have a director with that expertise. The statement should be done in consultation with the executive director.

Policy

The mission of the Applied Research & Development International, Inc. is to strengthen the management and leadership of public benefit nonprofit organizations so they will have increased capacity to improve their communities and society.

ARDI accomplishes this mission through advocating the importance of effective management and leadership; broadening access to resources; integrating related knowledge from the governmental, for-profit, and nonprofit sectors; and developing and testing new management approaches.

To accomplish this mission, ARDI operates with the following values:

- ARDI will put the well-being of society and the nonprofit sector and the ability to service the public good above its own needs.
- ARDI will employ and promote collaborative, inclusive, and collegial processes.
- ARDI will actively seek to avoid duplication and waste of efforts so that the resources of the nonprofit sector are used to greater impact.
- ARDI will employ the highest standards of management and leadership in its own organization.

As part of the strategy, our personnel policies, practices, and programs must:

- Attract qualified employees.
- Seek out highly motivated individuals who demonstrate an exceptional potential for success.
- Encourage the mentality of "self-starters" and individual responsibility.

- Design a compensation program that reflects internal equity and external market.
- Promote efficient management of ARDI resources.
- Remain flexible yet consistent by maintaining stability in senior management and administrative personnel.
- Offer intern opportunities that add value and support the operations of ARDI and at the same time meet the learning goals of students.
- Acknowledge that project specific personnel may experience turnover based on funding.

Recruiting and Compensation

- ARDI believes in hiring the most qualified people available and, whenever possible and appropriate, in promoting from within the ARDI staff. For each position, we will identify the required characteristics and fill the position with a person possessing the necessary skills.
- ARDI attempts to recruit people who are team-oriented and demonstrate leadership qualities.
- ARDI provides a supportive environment that encourages employees to take advantage of opportunities for personal and professional development.

Compensation

- ARDI believes in a total compensation program that is market-based and helps attract and retain a high quality workforce.
- ARDI believes our compensation program should reward employees who contribute to our commitment to excellence.
- ARDI believes the compensation level for each job should be established through an objective analysis.

Benefits

- ARDI believes benefits are an important component of the total compensation package.

Performance Management and Training

- ARDI believes there must be a consistent performance management process throughout ARDI; however, the performance measures may vary based on the level or nature of the job.

- The performance management process should include ongoing discussion between employees and supervisors, and should include both informal and formal evaluation processes.
- ARDI believes both results and efforts toward achieving results are important and that results should be measured against job standards and performance goals.

Communications

- ARDI believes in the importance of open, honest, respectful, and regular communication among all members of our organization.
- ARDI believes communication includes listening as well as talking. We expect and encourage employees to express opinions and offer suggestions to improve ARDI and increase our impact.

Human Resource Program Administration

- ARDI strives for simplicity in design and administration.
- ARDI believes in providing general policy guidelines to ensure human resource programs are consistently applied, but also in giving management sufficient flexibility to deal with special situations.
- ARDI does not discriminate in employment practices, career growth or other opportunities on the basis of race, sex, sexual preference, ethnicity, religion, national origin, marital status, age, disability, or veteran status.[1]

HUMAN RESOURCE MISSION STATEMENT

Rationale

This policy is based on the understanding that each department of an organization has an essential mission of its own to fulfill in support of the mission of the entire organization. In the example that follows, the organization has not only defined the departmental mission but also identified the key strategies by which the department accomplishes its mission. Several benefits flow from this policy. First, it identifies for each employee within the department that his or her work is essential to the good of the whole. Likewise, it identifies, for all members of the organization's community, how the department contributes to their well-being. The outcome from this is improved employee morale and a sense of interconnectedness. A second benefit of this policy is that it provides a basis for accountability that is useful for evaluation of achievement and administration of compensation is provided.

Policy

The University of Denver's Division of Human Resource commits to fostering a community of excellence through strategic leadership and service of the highest quality.

We accomplish this by:

- Developing and supporting an environment that assists the University community to recruit and retain quality faculty and staff.
- Providing personal and professional development opportunities for employees to realize their full potential in the workplace.
- Providing information management systems that support effective decision making at the University.[2]

CHAIN OF COMMAND

Rationale

It is important to clarify interaction between staff and board members to avoid confusion and undermining of the authority of the executive. A policy that clearly describes the proper chain of command is an important tool as it defines the expectations for board/staff communication through the executive.

The executive is hired by and accountable to the board. The executive then is charged with the design of the organization staffing structure and the jobs that comprise it. Boards or their committees may have input and may even retain the right of approval of the overall staffing structure and job design. At the very least, boards should be informed about the staffing structure and the jobs.

However, the executive is solely responsible for hiring and supervision of staff members within the policies approved by the board. The organization chart will show the supervision chain of command. Staff persons must work within this structure, taking issues to their supervisors and then to the executive director. Staff members are entitled to take concerns directly to the board only as defined by the grievance policy in the personnel policies or when the issues are still unresolved at the executive director level. The chairperson of the board can make this policy clear to board members and periodically reiterate it and hold board members accountable for following it, should employees take concerns directly to board members in "end runs" around the chain of command. In addition, executives can emphasize to staff persons that they are required to follow the chain of command in communicating their concerns. This policy is not intended to stifle staff concerns but rather to be sure that they are taken to supervisors who are most likely to be able to address them successfully. It also helps to ensure that the board role does not interfere with management's role.

This policy does not prohibit board and staff working together on committees and projects; nor does it prohibit staff members attending and participating in assigned roles in board meetings. The key is that the authorization of that participation comes from the executive, and it is expected that the authorized staff communication with the board is related to the assigned duties.

Policy

The board of directors of this nonprofit is responsible for setting policies for the organization. The board employs the executive director, to whom it delegates responsibility for the day-to-day administration of the nonprofit. The executive director manages the staff, using policies approved by the board of directors.

This nonprofit's staff members report to the executive director or the delegated manager. All communication to the board is channeled through the executive director, who may assign duties to staff persons in support of the board committees. A staff person who does not follow the stated policy of channeling information through the executive director is subject to disciplinary action.

OPEN DOOR

Rationale

An open door policy means that the executive and other managers are accessible and staff are welcome to express their views or concerns to them. It is expected that staff persons who report to managers other than the executive will take their issues to their supervisor first in most circumstances. Speaking with the supervisor may be enough, or a staff person may wish to also speak directly to the executive. An open door policy does not mean that the executive or managers must immediately interrupt their schedule to see the staff person. Rather it means that they are open to hearing the staff person's concerns. It is good to respond to requests for communication as soon as possible. At a minimum, the staff person should be given a definite time and date when he or she can be heard, and that time should be honored.

One benefit of this policy is improved morale, as staff will feel important and respected when they know that their supervisors and the executive are open to their input. A second benefit is that the organization gains from the knowledge and wisdom of staff and problems can be identified and acted on at early stages. Finally, such a policy provides an outlet for frustrations, which are a safety valve that may prevent escalation of employee dissatisfaction or development of more serious problems for the organization. According to the Nonprofit Risk Management Center (www.nonprofitrisk.com), insurance carriers and defense lawyers recommend that every employer have some sort of internal procedure for resolving complaints. Employee surveys may be one method for obtaining employee input that will help management gain information helpful to creating a motivating work environment (see Exhibits 1.1 and 1.2). Soliciting suggestions from employees is also a proactive way for employers to gain from employee ideas and for employees to raise concerns and issues and make suggestions for improvement.

Policy

EXHIBIT 1.1   EMPLOYEE SURVEYS

Example Employee Survey, Cover Memo, and Survey

To: All Employees

From: Executive Director

Date:

Subject: Employee Survey

You are a valuable part of this organization and we are interested in getting your feedback on your experiences as an employee. Your response will remain anonymous and results will only be shared with management and the board in a summarized form. Your input along with that of your fellow employees will guide this organization in the improvement of its human resource management system.

(continues)

EXHIBIT I.I   CONTINUED

Please complete this form sharing your individual opinion only and return it to
_____ by _____ date.

Thank you for your contributions to this organization and for taking the time to share your thoughts with us.

Employee Survey

Personal Data

Check One:

Sex

- ☐ Male
- ☐ Female

Age

- ☐ Under 21
- ☐ 21–29
- ☐ 30–39
- ☐ 40–49
- ☐ 50–59
- ☐ Over 60

Marital Status

- ☐ Married
- ☐ Single
- ☐ Single with dependents

Employment Data

Length of Service

- ☐ Less than 6 months
- ☐ 6 months–less than 1 year
- ☐ 1 year–less than 2 years
- ☐ 2 years–less than 3 years
- ☐ 3 years–less than 5 years
- ☐ 5 years–less than 10 years
- ☐ More than 10 years

EXHIBIT 1.1   CONTINUED

Hours worked per week

☐ Fewer than 20

☐ 20–30

☐ 31–39

☐ 40 or more

Job Category

☐ Exempt

☐ Nonexempt

Directions: Rate the following aspects of your job from 1 (low) to 5 (high).

1. Leadership. How satisfied are you with the effectiveness of the organization's leadership?

_____ Satisfaction

Add your comments regarding the organization's leadership:

2. Supervision. How satisfied are you with the supervision you receive?

_____ Satisfaction

Add your comments regarding the supervision you receive:

3. Compensation. Do you believe you are appropriately compensated for your work?

_____ Yes _____ No

Add your comments regarding the compensation for your work:

4. Benefits. Your current benefits include (insert list of benefits offered, the list might include, for example, health insurance 80% company paid for employee, family coverage that employee pays is optional, retirement, life insurance, dental insurance, prescription drug plan, and disability insurance. Paid leave benefits include: 10 vacation days per year, 1 sick day is accrued monthly with 30 maximum, 10 paid holidays, and 2 personal leave days per year.) How satisfied are you with the benefits you receive?

_____ Satisfaction

Add your comments regarding the benefits plan:

(continues)

EXHIBIT I.I   CONTINUED

5. Polices and Procedures. How satisfied are you with the clarity and completeness of the personnel policies?

_____ Satisfaction

Add your comments regarding the personnel policies:

6. Communication. How do you rate the communication of the information about the organization, particularly as it affects your ability to do your job?

_____ Satisfaction

Add your comments regarding communications:

7. Career. How do you rate your ability to advance your career within the organization?

_____ Satisfaction

Add your comments regarding career advancement:

8. Training. How do you rate the training and education opportunities offered?

_____ Satisfaction

Add your comments regarding training opportunities:

9. Performance Evaluation. How satisfied are you with the timeliness and fairness of the performance evaluation you receive?

_____ Satisfaction

Add your comments regarding performance evaluations:

10. What other comments would you like to make regarding your experience as an employee for this organization?

EXHIBIT 1.2   EMPLOYEE SURVEY COVER LETTER

Memorandum

TO: All [Nonprofit's name] staff

FROM: Executive Director

DATE:

REGARDING: Employee survey

Attached is an employee survey that is designed to give you an opportunity for input into decision making that affects your employment.

We have undertaken this survey because you are a valuable part of our team, and we want to gain understanding from staff as to how we can develop increased ability to recruitment and retain top-quality staff.

Your responses to this survey will stay anonymous. We will collate the results and share them with the board of directors. We will use the results to make decisions regarding the human resource management policies and procedures.

Fill out this survey completely. Send your completed survey to the attention of [Name].

Thank you for your thoughtful cooperation!

RETURN BY: insert date

SUGGESTIONS

Rationale

Staff members should be encouraged to make suggestions directly to their supervisors and in meetings. Sometimes, however, they may be reluctant. Staff members might share their suggestions in writing if a suggestion box is available. It is good to encourage staff members to contribute their ideas, which may be valuable to the organization. There is a secondary benefit to encouraging staff members to use the suggestion box: It provides a sanctioned channel through which they can express themselves, which may be healthier than for issues to build up with no outlet.

The policy should state that staff suggestions are valued and that suggestions will be given careful consideration. The policy should explain how suggestions should be submitted; for example, using a form that staff members can complete and give to their supervisors or that they can place in a suggestion box. It should specify whether signed suggestions will be responded to and in what manner.

Policy

Suggestions from staff members are always welcomed and will be given thoughtful consideration. The proper method of making suggestions is in writing to your supervisor. Suggestion forms (see Exhibit 1.3) can be picked up at the main office.

EXHIBIT 1.3   EMPLOYEE SUGGESTION FORM

This nonprofit encourages its staff members to write their suggestions and give them to their supervisor. If you would like to make a suggestion, please complete this form.

1. What suggestion would you like to make?

2. Please explain the effect your suggestion would have on the workplace. For example, tell us how it would improve services or a program, save money, help staff morale, improve teamwork, etc.

Employee's Signature (optional)	Date
Supervisor's Signature	Date

Action—Supervisor only

ADMINISTRATOR ON DUTY

Rationale

This policy is especially important for organizations that have services and facilities in use beyond regular weekday business hours. It provides staff with a chain of command to follow when a situation or problem comes up that requires a management decision when no manager is immediately available. Such a policy should state why an administrator on duty is needed, give examples of crisis or emergency situations, and explain when and how staff members can contact the administrator on duty.

Policy

From time to time, an emergency or other situation that requires a management decision must be made when no administrator is on duty. To make it possible for staff to contact an administrator in this situation, this nonprofit has an administrator on duty program.

An administrator will be available by pager, for emergencies, from 4:30 PM on Friday until 8 AM on Monday. Emergency situations can include anything that could endanger the health, safety, or welfare of staff, volunteers, or people the nonprofit serves. In a medical emergency, staff should always call 9-1-1 first, then the administrator on duty. Emergency situations where a management decision is required include, but are not limited to: severe behavior, any involvement with legal authorities, theft, or vandalism. On the assigned weekend, the administrator on duty will be responsible for carrying a pager and responding to calls from staff. Staff members will be given the pager number and procedures for using it.

Crisis Response Team

Rationale

A small team should be formed to coordinate a nonprofit's response to a crisis. The team should be formed and trained in preparation for possible crises. The composition and size of the team should be tailored to each individual nonprofit, identifying the most likely source of a crisis and being sure that the team has the right mix of expertise. The executive director is a likely person to include on the team and may chair it. The executive director's position gives him or her the authority to make decisions and command the respect and attention needed from others. Often executive directors are already serving as the organization spokesperson and can do so as needed during the crisis. Other types of talent that may be needed include legal, accounting, and project manager. The board or outside experts may be drawn from to form the team. The Nonprofit Risk Management Center (www.nonprofitrisk.com) provided an article on this subject in its archived newsletter and refers to the book, *Vital Signs: Anticipating, Preventing and Surviving a Crisis in a Nonprofit* by Melanie L. Herman and Barbara B. Oliver.

Explanation of Personnel Policies, Changes, or Revisions

Rationale

Personnel polices should be reviewed routinely each year or when experience in the organization or a change of employment laws and regulations may require an update. When changes are made, it is important to make sure those changes are communicated to employees. This can be done in writing as an addendum to the existing policies as a temporary measure, if the change occurs during the year, or entire revised personnel policies can be issued. It is also important to discuss the changes during staff meetings or in memos to staff members.

Staff members should sign an acknowledgment form stating that they have read and understand the new policies. This acknowledgment form should be kept in their personnel file with the one they signed when they were hired.

Authority to establish and change personnel policies rests solely with the board of directors of the nonprofit. Policies may be changed at any time, with or without notice—and then, only in writing, by the nonprofit's board of directors.

Roundtable Meetings

Rationale

Managers can gain valuable information and improve employee morale by listening to employees. Roundtable meetings or discussion sessions between managers and employees are a good forum for hearing employee viewpoints either on key issues identified by the manager or as an open forum to learn what is on employees' minds. Some procedural considerations are: How will the meetings be announced? Who will be chosen to attend, or is attendance based on self-selection? How many people will be allowed to attend the meetings? Will the topic be preannounced if chosen by the manager? What is the purpose of the roundtable meeting? Do attendees need to submit their issues in advance? How long will the meetings be?

It is important that the degree of power of attendees is made clear. For example, attendees may be invited to comment on a pending new merit-based compensation program under consideration by top management, but top management will make the final recommendations on the program for action by the board of directors. Or, for example, an employee suggests starting a book exchange program and employees receive authorization in the meeting to proceed as they see fit.

Policy

Roundtable meetings are designed to allow two-way communication between top management and staff members of the nonprofit. The executive director hosts these events. The executive director is the only representative of senior management present. Attendees are selected in a random manner, by grade, from all the departments in the nonprofit. Most meetings will have 12 attendees.

Roundtable meetings will allow staff members an opportunity to address issues of concern, present views on topics of interest, and exchange ideas and information. These meetings are not designed to be gripe sessions, but rather as a vehicle to discuss significant issues with the intent of improving the overall performance of the organization and the work environment.

Roundtable meetings are held once a quarter. A week prior to the meeting date, each prospective attendee will receive a personal invitation with an RSVP date. At this time, prospective attendees are encouraged to submit questions or suggestions for discussion items in writing to the executive director.

PROBLEM-SOLVING PROCEDURE

Rationale

Interpersonal conflicts and problems are inevitable in the workplace. Most can and should be solved at the lowest level of supervision, but some will need to go on to a higher management level. A policy is needed that clearly identifies the levels, steps, time periods, and methods for official problem-solving procedures and provides protection for the organization, managers, and involved employees. The U.S. Supreme Court determined that when there was a complaint mechanism at the workplace that a sexual harassment victim did not take advantage of, the employer has an affirmative defense to a lawsuit. The reasoning was that if the plaintiff really felt harassed, the employee would have taken advantage of the employer's grievance procedures. This type of reasoning also has been used to challenge plaintiff claims regarding employment law violations. Thus, having an internal grievance mechanism not only helps employee relations but also is a basic risk management procedure for nonprofits. The goal is to allow problems to be resolved at the lowest level possible so legal actions are not taken. Employees who use the grievance process should be guaranteed that they will not be retaliated against.

Policy

Grievance Policy   Employees may use the grievance procedure by submitting complaints to their supervisor in written form within 10 working days of the incident or situation that the grievance pertains to. (In the case when the grievance directly concerns the employee's supervisor, the complaint may be submitted to the executive director.) The supervisor or executive director will respond to the complaint within 7 working days of its receipt. If the employee is not satisfied with the response of the supervisor, he or she may request a review by the executive director. The executive director has 10 working days to respond in writing to the grievance.

If the employee is still not satisfied, he or she can ask for a review of the response of the supervisor and executive director by a committee of the board of directors. This request must be submitted in writing to the board chairperson within 5 days of receiving the executive director's response. The board chairperson will appoint a task force or committee to review the complaint, and it will respond within 10 working days of having received the complaint. The ruling of the board is final. An employee will not be retaliated against for using the grievance procedure.

SPEAKING WITH THE MEDIA

Rationale

A single spokesperson for the organization should be identified. In many organizations, that person is the executive director. For other organizations, it may be a communications officer. When there is no executive staff leader, the president of the board often fulfills the spokesperson role. It is appropriate to designate a staff spokesperson but also to have agreement with the board about which board member will speak when board-level comments are appropriate.

A major benefit of having a single individual give information to the news media is that stories will be more consistent and accurate and reflect an official position rather than personal opinion.

Policy

All inquiries from the media should be referred to the executive director unless the director has identified a designate for a specific matter. The executive director will refer the inquiry to the chairperson of the board when board-level comments are appropriate.

PRESS RELEASES

Rationale

Press releases are a tool for the nonprofit organization to use in creating a public image, for visibility, and to respond to issues. A policy is needed about when and by whom press releases are written and who has the authority to approve and release them. The executive director often retains this control. If the release might generate controversy, it is a good idea to share it with the appropriate board leaders in advance.

REFERENCES

1. clb & associates, Carol L. Barbeito, Ph.D., 5793 Jasper Point Circle, Castle Rock, CO 80108.
2. Department of Human Resources University of Denver, 2199 S. University Boulevard, Denver, CO 80208.

CHAPTER 2

Nondiscrimination

This chapter contains information and policies that will help position nonprofits to avoid discrimination and keep them in compliance with civil rights laws and nondiscrimination laws.

EQUAL EMPLOYMENT OPPORTUNITY AND AFFIRMATIVE ACTION

Rationale

Nonprofit organizations with 50 or more staff and income of more than $50,000 from the federal government need to write an affirmative action policy and develop an affirmative action plan. All nonprofits might consider having such policies and plans as a reflection of their value system, which may include a commitment to achieving diversity among the people working for and with their organization. While the law pertains to paid staff, nonprofits should consider similar efforts to achieve diversity among their volunteers including the board of directors and even vendors and clients.

An affirmative action plan is a detailed outline of strategies the nonprofit uses to attract minorities. It supports the policy statement on affirmative action but remains separate from it.

Although most policies are only a few paragraphs long, some can be quite detailed, and may involve advice from an attorney. An affirmative action plan typically includes: assessments of the workforce, available pool of workers, specific recruitment procedures, references to training and promotion, implementation plans, a statement about record keeping, and a complaint procedure. Nonprofits that operate under affirmative action plans also must file periodic compliance reports with the federal Equal Employment Opportunity Commission.

Unlike an affirmative action plan, an equal employment opportunity (EEO) statement does not require extensive development and documentation. It is simply a statement of the nonprofit's commitment to equal opportunity in employment and intent to abide by civil rights laws.

The law does allow exclusion of certain protected groups, but only in rare instances and only if it can be proven that exclusion is based on a bona fide occupational qualification (BFOQ). If there are any questions about this or any other hiring issue, check with an attorney to find out what state and federal guidelines allow.

The benefits of having diverse people involved with the nonprofit can go well beyond issues of compliance with the law and public relations. Diversity that reflects the client base helps to ensure the programs are relevant and culturally accessible. Different viewpoints can contribute to wiser decisions. Morally and ethically, the organization will be on firmer ground with well-crafted and implemented equal opportunity and affirmative action policies.

Policy

Equal Employment Opportunity Statement   This nonprofit believes that equal opportunity for all staff members is important for the continuing success of our organization. In accordance with state and federal law, this nonprofit will not discriminate against a staff member or applicant for employment because of race, disability, color, creed, religion, sex, sexual orientation, age, national origin, ancestry, citizenship, veteran status, or non–job-related factors in hiring, promoting, demoting, training, benefits, transfers, layoffs, terminations, recommendations, rates of pay, or other forms of compensation. Opportunity is provided to all staff members based on qualifications and job requirements.

Affirmative Action Statement   This nonprofit provides equal employment opportunity to all persons without regard to race, color, religion, disability, sex, sexual orientation, age, national origin, ancestry, citizenship, veteran status, or non–job-related factors, and promotes the full realization of this policy through a positive, continuing program of affirmative action. This nonprofit is committed to equal opportunity for all applicants and staff members in personnel matters including recruitment and hiring, benefits, training, promotion, compensation, transfer, and layoff or termination. We strive for a staff that reflects diversity.

We will attempt to achieve and maintain a diverse workforce. These steps may include, but are not limited to:

- Pursue our affirmative action program along with regular review by the board of directors
- Ensure that this nonprofit's policy regarding equal employment opportunity is communicated to all staff persons
- Ensure that hiring, promotion, and salary administration practices are fair and consistent with the policy of the nonprofit
- Report to the board of directors on all activities and efforts to implement the nonprofit's policy of equal employment opportunities
- Make special recruitment efforts as part of this plan, to the extent that our staff is not diverse

Each supervisor and member of the management staff must provide equal opportunity for all staff members with regard to work assignments, training, transfer, advancement, and other conditions and privileges of employment, and work to assure a continuation of this policy of equal employment opportunity.

ADA COMPLIANCE

Rationale

Compliance with the Americans with Disabilities Act (ADA) is a must for all nonprofit organizations. It is mandatory to post notices about ADA in the office and to make sure employees are informed about the act. A disability is defined as:

- A physical or mental impairment that substantially limits one or more of the major life activities of such individual
- A record of such impairment
- Being regarded as having such an impairment

Recent U.S. Supreme Court rulings provide that if an individual is able to mitigate fully the effects of the disability, that individual may not be protected by the ADA.

ADA affects a number of hiring and employment practices. These forms of discrimination, among others, are illegal under ADA:

- Limiting the duties of a staff person with a disability based on a presumption about what is best for the person or the individual's ability to perform certain tasks

- Adopting separate lines of advancement for staff members with disabilities, based on the presumption that no one with a disability would be interested in moving into a particular job

- Denying employment to an applicant based on generalized fears about the safety of the applicant or higher rates of absenteeism

- Denying a job, promotion, or benefits to an individual without a disability because he or she has a relationship or association with a person with a disability

- Denying employment opportunities to a qualified applicant or staff person based on the need to make reasonable accommodations

- Administering tests in a manner that fails to accurately reflect the skills, aptitude, or other factors intended to be measured

- Participating in contractual or other relationships that subject a qualified applicant or staff member with a disability to discrimination that is prohibited by the ADA

- Using standards, criteria, or methods of administration that discriminate because of a disability

- Failing to make reasonable accommodations for the known physical or mental limitations of a qualified applicant or staff person with a disability, unless it can be demonstrated that the accommodation imposes an undue hardship for the nonprofit

In some cases, nonprofits may ask job applicants whether they will need reasonable accommodations to perform the job and, if so, what type of accommodations. As an employer, these questions may be asked if:

- It is reasonable to believe the applicant will need reasonable accommodation because of an obvious disability,

- It is reasonable to believe the applicant will need reasonable accommodation because of a hidden disability that the applicant has voluntarily disclosed, or

- An applicant has voluntarily disclosed that reasonable accommodation for the job is needed.

For a free copy of these guidelines, write to: Office of Community Affairs, EEOC, 1801 L Street NW, Washington, DC 20507. To order by phone, call 800-669-4000. Ask for ADA Enforcement Guidance: Pre-employment Disability-Related Questions and Medical Examinations. This document also can be downloaded from the EEOC's Web site at www.eeoc.gov/docs/preemp.html.

Medical information about employees with disabilities may be needed for emergency purposes. Such information should be safeguarded by keeping it separate from the staff person's personnel file, putting it in a separate envelope marked "confidential" and keeping the files locked.

Policy

This nonprofit welcomes applications from people with disabilities and does not discriminate against them in any way. This nonprofit complies with the Americans with Disabilities Act of 1990 by:

- Considering all applicants with disabilities for employment using the same criteria as are used for the employment of persons without disabilities

- Considering staff persons with disabilities for promotion using the same criteria that are used for the promotion of staff persons without disabilities

- Taking steps to make its facilities barrier-free and accessible according to appropriate federal and state statutes

- Making scheduling and other adjustments to reasonably accommodate staff members with disabilities

- Educating staff persons to the fact that employees with disabilities should not be discriminated against

- Posting notices explaining the provisions of ADA and staff rights under the law

SEXUAL HARASSMENT

Rationale

Every nonprofit should adopt and enforce a policy against sexual harassment that covers employees, volunteers, and indeed every person interacting with the organization. The policy can provide a shield of liability and avoid escalation of a problem. Of even greater importance is that harassing behavior has grave consequences of undermining morale, interference with productivity, and reducing public support. In November 1993 the U.S. Supreme Court ruled that a staff member does not have to show proof of severe psychological harm to collect damages in a sexual harassment lawsuit. Instead, the Court ruled that all that must be shown is that a reasonable person would be offended by the situation and that it interferes with the person's ability to do his or her work. The effect of this new ruling is to put all employers on notice that a workplace where sexual joking, innuendoes, or sexually offensive comments are tolerated could result in their being sued.

The Court, in effect, said that employers must make an effort to educate their staff and volunteers about the organization's policy and encourage staff and volunteers to come forward with complaints of sexual harassment.

Appropriate policies and practices start with the board of directors. The board adopts an emphatic policy that states a commitment to creating and maintaining a harassment-free workplace. The board should not only establish the written policy but ask the executive director to provide periodic reports on how the policy is distributed so all employees are aware of it. All complaints should be brought to the attention of the executive director. The board should receive reports on complaints under the policy and their dispositions. Protection of the privacy of all parties should be included in the procedures. Zero tolerance and disciplinary action against perpetrators should be expected.

The policy should cover these behaviors:

- Unwelcome sexual advances
- Requests for sexual acts or favors
- Insulting or degrading sexual remarks or conduct directed against another staff person; threats, demands, or suggestions that a staff person's work is contingent on toleration of or acquiescence to sexual advances

- Retaliation against staff members for complaining about such behaviors
- Any other unwelcome statements or actions based on sex that are sufficiently severe or pervasive so as to unreasonably interfere with an individual's work performance or create an intimidating, hostile, or offensive working environment

Complaints of sexual harassment should be investigated as promptly as possible. The allegations of the complaint and the identity of the persons involved shall remain confidential, in order to conduct a full and impartial investigation, remedy violations, monitor compliance, and administer the policy.

The investigation will include, but will not be limited to, discussion with both parties and witnesses.

AIDS

Rationale

Persons with HIV/AIDS are covered by the Americans with Disabilities Act. It is illegal to fire a staff person who tests positive for HIV or to ask about a job applicant's HIV status during an interview.

In addition, the law prohibits discrimination against staff members or job applicants because they associate with known HIV and/or AIDS carriers. Employers who discriminate against people who have HIV are liable for compensatory and punitive damages and risk losing their federal funding.

Given ADA restrictions, the only instance in which action against current staff members or job candidates can be taken is when their condition prohibits them from fulfilling essential job functions.

AIDS is a devastating disease, and the organization will want to be sure to make every attempt to provide a caring, supportive environment for these individuals. Staff members should be educated about the nature of AIDS and how it is, and is not, transmitted.

Policy

AIDS, or acquired immune deficiency syndrome, is a disease caused by a virus that does not survive well outside the human body. Research has shown that AIDS is a very difficult disease to catch because it is not spread by casual contact. Since it was first identified in the United States in 1981, medical scientists have ascertained that AIDS is transmitted most often in two ways: (1) through sexual contact, or (2) through sharing contaminated intravenous needles. Infected mothers also can pass AIDS to their unborn babies. There is very little risk of catching AIDS from a coworker in the normal course of business relations.

Therefore, this nonprofit will not discriminate against people who have AIDS or those with the human immunodeficiency virus (HIV) that usually leads to AIDS. Staff members and persons served by this nonprofit may not legally be denied access to services or terminated from their jobs because of their AIDS condition. This nonprofit also will strive to provide a caring, supportive environment for staff members or persons it serves with AIDS.

Reasonable Accommodation

Rationale

The Americans with Disabilities Act requires that reasonable accommodations be made for staff members with disabilities (see Exhibit 2.1).

An organization policy on ADA should state the employer's rights, including that employers retain the final judgment call on reasonable accommodations for disabilities; as long as the accommodations are effective.

EEOC Policy Guidance on Reasonable Accommodation

The following guidelines can help you understand the requirements of the Americans with Disabilities Act (ADA) regarding reasonable accommodations.

On March 1, 1999 the Equal Employment Opportunity Commission released Enforcement Guidance on Reasonable Accommodation and Undue Hardship under the Americans with Disabilities Act. This guidance is intended to clarify issues concerning reasonable accommodation. And while EEOC guidance doesn't have the force of law, courts can refer to it in legal decisions.

Requesting a Reasonable Accommodation

Staff persons must request a reasonable accommodation by informing their employer that they need an adjustment or change at work for a reason related to a medical condition. These requests need not be in writing and can be in ordinary English; for example, staff members are not required to use the words "reasonable accommodation." If the nonprofit believes that the need for reasonable accommodation or the disability is not obvious, the nonprofit may ask the staff member for medical documentation.

Who Decides the Reasonable Accommodation?

An employer does not have to offer the specific accommodation the staff person requests. Instead, it can choose one that is less costly or easier to provide. The accommodation, however, must be effective. The nonprofit must also respond promptly to requests for accommodation.

Some Examples of Reasonable Accommodations

A reasonable accommodation may be job restructuring, unpaid leave, modified duty or part-time schedule, physical adjustments to the workplace, or reassigning staff persons to a vacant position for which they have the skill qualifications and can perform the essential functions with or without reasonable accommodation. Reassignments should be to positions that are as comparable in pay and status as possible if the equivalent position is not vacant.

What Is Not a Reasonable Accommodation?

An employer need not help a staff person become qualified, bump another staff member, create a position, or promote the staff person who has a disability. Employers do not have to eliminate a primary job responsibility, provide personal use items, or excuse violations of a uniformly applied rule of conduct.

Communication

An employer may not tell other staff members that a coworker is receiving a reasonable accommodation. The ADA strictly limits the disclosure of medical information, and such a statement may constitute a disclosure of disability. When staff members ask why a coworker appears to be receiving

(continues)

different treatment, an employer can say it has a policy on assisting staff members and on respecting their privacy. Employers also can ask staff persons with a known disability if a reasonable accommodation is needed and if those staff members reasonably believe they may need such an accommodation. An employer can ask a staff member with a known disability who is having performance or conduct problems if a reasonable accommodation is needed.

Undue Hardship

To claim that a suggested accommodation would cause an undue hardship, an employer must look at the nature and cost of the accommodation and the overall financial resources of the nonprofit. An undue hardship may not, however, be influenced by the perceptions of staff members or others about the accommodated staff person, or because providing such an accommodation may have a negative effect on morale. Undue hardship may occur when an accommodation is unduly disruptive to other staff members' ability to work.[1]

Policy

EXHIBIT 2.1   REQUEST FOR ACCOMMODATION

Type of Accommodation Requested: _____

_____

_____

_____

_____

_____

Essential Functions of Job: (to be completed by employee's supervisor) _____

_____

_____

_____

_____

_____

EXHIBIT 2.1   CONTINUED

Accommodation Granted: Yes _____

                         No _____

Nonprofit's Decision with Respect to Requested Accommodation: _____

_____

_____

_____

Resources Used: _____

_____

_____

_____

If Accommodation Was Denied, Why?: _____

_____

_____

_____

_____

Alternate Accommodation Suggested? Outcome?: _____

_____

_____

Result of Determination Discussed with the Employee and Supervisor: _____

Comments:_____

_____

_____

_____   _____

Employee's Signature   Date   Supervisor's Signature   Date

_____   _____

Executive Director's Signature   Date[2]

ANTIHARASSMENT

Rationale

Adopting a harassment policy that extends coverage to everyone in the non-profit makes clear that the organization is committed to a workplace that is free of harassment of any kind.

An antiharassment policy can include sexual and other types of harassment policy. It can state the reporting procedure for those who feel that they have been unlawfully harassed and actively encourage staff members who feel they have been victims of unlawful harassment to complain.

Equally important is a statement that the nonprofit will take action on staff members' complaints and that it will not retaliate against them for making a complaint or tolerate any retaliation directed toward them by others.

Policy

This nonprofit prohibits disparate and unfair treatment of any staff member or individual on the basis of race, color, sex, sexual orientation, religion, national origin, age, disability, or marital status. This treatment includes harassment and intimidation, whether physical or verbal. Harassment is behavior perceived by the receiver as unwelcome and includes, but is not limited to, the use of verbal or practical jokes, unwelcome touching, offensive remarks or put-downs, gestures, or displays of objects and materials that create an offensive environment.

If you feel you are the victim of harassment in any form, you are encouraged to discuss the matter with your supervisor or directly with the executive director.

The executive director will proceed with an investigation of the claim in a prompt and discreet manner. On the basis of the investigation, the executive director will make a decision in writing as soon as possible after completing the investigation. The decision shall state if there is a finding of harassment and what action the nonprofit will take to remedy the situation. A copy of the written decision will be given to the individual who made the complaint.

This nonprofit will not tolerate intimidation, coercion, or discrimination of any kind against staff persons or other individuals who file complaints or who testify, assist, or participate in any manner in an investigation or hearing. All such acts against complainants or other participants should be reported immediately to the executive director.

In those cases where retaliation can be established, the executive director may take disciplinary action up to and including dismissal.

References

1. Equal Employment Opportunity Commission, "Enforcement Guidance on Reasonable Accommodation and Undue Hardship under the Americans with Disabilities Act," 1999, Washington, DC.
2. Ibid.

CHAPTER 3

Recruitment, Hiring, and Termination

This chapter provides policies that will aid the nonprofit in recruitment, hiring, and termination of employees.

RECRUITMENT

HIRING POLICY

Rationale

A nonprofit's success depends on the quality of its staff. Therefore, a well-thought-out and carried-out recruitment process is vital. A recruitment policy that ensures that the hiring procedures are consistent and fair to everyone is important.

Preference for Internal Candidates   Benefits occur from giving existing staff members the first consideration when a position is vacated or a new position created. Morale and productivity may be improved and the agency may have greater success in recruiting high-quality new staff. Because most nonprofits are small to medium-size organizations, development of a career path can be very challenging. Giving existing staff members first consideration when an opening occurs is one way to address this challenge. Hiring appropriately qualified existing staff members has advantages as they are already knowledgeable about the organization and their skills and fit within the organization and with other staff members are known.

In one type of preference for internal candidates' policy, the position is first advertised in-house only. External recruitment is conducted when the determination is made that there are no qualified internal candidates. Another version is when internal candidates have the option to apply and may be given some special consideration in the hiring process, but the position is posted in-house and externally at the same time. This policy is obviously less preferential, but still offers existing staff members the opportunity to compete. It is more work to advertise externally, however, if the goal is to move the search for the best candidate along rapidly, and it is not clear the best candidates exist in-house, then simultaneous advertising may be wise.

Testing/Screening/Interviewing   The processes for testing, screening, and interviewing should be established in advance and care should be taken that they are followed for all applicants. It is wise to document carefully the time of receipt of application, the process followed, and the results of the process for each candidate.

If applicants are required to complete a standard application form or take a job-related test, be prepared to make adjustments to accommodate those with disabilities. The Americans with Disabilities Act requires that an applicant's special needs be taken into consideration. Examples of such accommodation are large print, sign language assistance, and accessible interview site.

References   Three references are generally asked for. If the candidate does not have three work-related references, character and business references, such as clergy, banks, or membership associations should be requested. Nonprofits should call each candidate's references, but tread cautiously here. Contacting a former employer against an applicant's wishes may create vulnerability. However, asking job candidates to sign a reference waiver eliminates risk. If applicants refuse to sign the waiver, they may be disqualified from consideration.

Some states allow employers to review police records. Doing so may be wise if an applicant admits to having been convicted of a crime.

Policy

In-House and External Position Searches   Qualified persons from within this nonprofit will fill job openings when the internal candidate has at least as good as or better qualifications than an external candidate. Positive consideration will be given to the fact that internal candidates know the organization and to the performance record in former and current positions in the organization. Job openings and instructions for applying will be posted on the official office bulletin board and intra-office computer bulletin board. The posting will contain the position qualifications and state eligibility requirements, method of application, and application deadlines. At the discretion of executive management, a position search may begin externally at the same time as the internal job posting or the external search may be delayed until a determination that there are no qualified candidates in-house. If the position requires special skills or knowledge that executive management determines is not available in-house, only an external search will be conducted.

Testing/Screening   Applicants for certain positions may be required to fill out a standard screening instrument and take a test as a condition of being considered for employment. All such tools will not discriminate against race, color, religion, disability, sex, sexual orientation, age, or national origin.

Interviewing   Applicants will be screened to determine who should become candidates for a job. More than one person, including the position's supervisor, may interview job candidates.

References will be checked on all candidates to whom job offers may be made, before the offers are made. Depending on state laws, police record checks may also be required.

REQUISITION FOR NEW HIRE

Rationale

A requisition for new hire policy outlines the procedure to be followed for approval of a job posting. The policy details the process to be followed by supervisors who wish to fill a vacant or new position. When there is a human resource department, the requisition for new hire may be directed to it. In most nonprofits, the requisition will be directed to the executive director.

Having such a policy has several benefits. This approval process helps to ensure the job description is up to date and necessary. Another benefit is that someone with oversight and planning responsibility for the whole organization's human resources can check to be sure that the position is properly slotted in the organization chart and wage scales. Further, the person can make sure there is adequate funding in the budget for the new hire.

DEGREES, LICENSES, AND CERTIFICATION

Rationale

Because high school graduation, college degrees, license, or certification normally are required for a prospective hire to qualify for a position, it is usual for the candidate to be responsible for obtaining and supplying proof of graduation and degree award and/or that his or her license or certification is active. Likewise, it is common for employees to have the responsibility for maintaining their own license of certification and supplying proof to their employers. The employer may choose to assist a candidate or employee financially or through other support. The employee has the responsibility to notify the employer of any change of status affecting the license or certification. The employer would be wise to keep a tick system regarding timing for license or certification renewal to remind employees and obtain proof on a timely basis.

Policy

Employment candidates whose jobs require high school graduation, GED, advanced degrees, professional license, or certification must present documentation of these prior to employment.

Employees pay their own costs of obtaining their proof of graduation, transcripts, licenses, or certifications, and in the case of licenses or certifications, of maintaining them in good status.

Copies of the degree award, transcripts, licenses, or certifications plus copies of all renewal or changes must be provided by the staff person for inclusion in his or her personnel file.

Staff persons must notify their supervisors within one workday of any changes in the status of their license or certification.

NEPOTISM

Rationale

Combining work relationships and family relationships can cause problems. Family members are often suspected of favoritism, and family issues may spill over into the workplace. Many organizations have policies prohibiting nepotism (the hiring of family members) at least for permanent positions. In a larger organization, it may be possible to allow members of the same family to work in the organization in different departments, avoiding supervision of one family member by another. Definition of what constitutes a family member is wise and will avoid hiring disputes. Mother, father, husband, wife, children, and siblings are considered immediate family, although an organization may wish to include other family relationships. Be sure to check with an attorney regarding the state law on this as with other personnel policies.

Policy

This organization prohibits employment of more than one member of an immediate family, defined as mother, father, husband, wife, children, and siblings, in the same department except for short-term temporary duties. These policies are strictly prohibited:

- No staff person will be permitted to hire a relative.
- One relative may not supervise another relative.
- Related persons will not be involved in evaluating each other's job performance or in making recommendations for salary adjustments, promotions, or other budget decisions.

IMMIGRATION REFORM AND CONTROL ACT OF 1986

Rationale

The Immigration Reform and Control Act of 1986 requires employers to prove that their employees are U.S. citizens or are legally authorized to work in the United States. Employees hired or recruited for a fee after November 6, 1986 also are subject to a document inspection process to determine this status.

New employees must complete Immigration and Naturalization (INS) Form I-9 and produce documentation on work authorization or show proof of citizenship. It is wise to add a disclaimer in the policy stating that this information will be used for lawful purposes only.

Policy

The Immigration Reform and Control Act of 1986 requires that this nonprofit ensure that employees are authorized for employment in the United States. In connection with the Immigration Reform and Control Act of 1986, this nonprofit must collect certain information on INS Form I-9 and review certain documentation concerning the employment authorization of individuals hired after November 6, 1986. This information and documentation will be used only for compliance with the Immigration Reform and Control Act of 1986 and not for any unlawful purpose. If your employment authorization changes or terminates after the start date of your employment, please inform the executive director immediately.

CAREER OPPORTUNITY PROGRAM

Rationale

Opportunities for career advancement are important motivators for many staff members. During the recruitment process, many applicants will want to know what opportunities exist for career advancement in the nonprofit organization. They may even state their own goals for advancement and want to know what the possibilities are within the organization that may help them meet their goals. A policy regarding career opportunity formalizes the organization's stance and communicates intent to support career development for employees. It might be wise to require that employees spend a specified period of time in the position for which they were hired before they are eligible for promotion. However, training and skill development can be made available and are one aspect of career development.

Hiring

At-Will Statement

Rationale

An "at-will" clause states that employees are free to terminate employment at any time and that the organization has the right to terminate their employment within the law. Many attorneys recommend this statement as a part of the personnel policies as protection against wrongful discharge lawsuits. However, some states do not recognize the validity of at-will policies as a defense in unlawful termination lawsuits. An attorney should know state law regarding at-will employment in the state. In states where at-will clauses are not recognized, "just cause" for termination must be proven if the organization is challenged. Just cause can include misconduct, incompetence, nonperformance, layoffs, and situations arising from institutional reorganization.

Policy

The staff member understands that employment at this nonprofit is at-will and of indefinite duration. Either the staff member or the nonprofit may terminate employment at any time, with or without notice and for any reason. No agreement to the contrary will be recognized unless such an agreement is in writing and signed by the executive director.

Receipt of Policy Manual

Rationale

New employees should receive their personnel polices manual on their first day of work. It is wise to have them sign and date a form that indicates they have received the manual and other orientation information. This receipt form should be kept in their personnel record. The receipt should state that employees understand it is their responsibility to read the manual and to ask their supervisor or human resource staff for clarification of any items they do not fully understand. Further, the receipt should state that the manual does not constitute an employment contract, either expressed or implied.

The manual informs employees of the policies regarding their employment as adopted by the board of directors and which the executive director is responsible for implementing. The organization has the right to change polices, which will be communicated in writing as an addendum to the manual. If there are extensive changes, a revised manual will be issued. When addendums or revised manuals are issued, it is important to have each employee sign a form similar to the one they signed as a new employee stating that he or she has received the revisions (see Exhibit 3.1).

Policy

EXHIBIT 3.1   RECEIPT OF POLICY MANUAL

I have received a copy of the Personnel Policies Manual and understand it is my responsibility to read and ensure I understand all polices and to ask my supervisor or a human resource staff person for clarification on items I do not understand. I agree that my employment can be terminated at-will. I understand that the board of directors has approved the policies in this manual. I know that policies may change, as the organization deems appropriate. I understand that I will be notified in writing of changes.

_____   _____
Employee Signature   Date

_____
Employee Name (printed)

_____   _____
Supervisor/Human Resource Staff Signature   Date

Receipt of Addendums

Title of Addendum	Date Received	Employee Signature
_____	_____	_____
_____	_____	_____

_____

INTRODUCTORY PERIOD

Rationale

An introductory period, often of 90 or 180 days, allows the employer to ensure that new hires successfully integrate into the organization and achieve the level of competent performance in their position appropriate to their time on the job, before they become regular employees. The wording in this policy is important. Be sure to state the length of the introductory period as up to the length of time, for example: "the introductory period is up to 90 days." This covers the situation in which the employer determines the employee needs to be terminated during the introductory period. Determine and be clear about employee eligibility for benefits during the introductory period, and state when and under what conditions benefits are provided.

The policy also should explain how satisfactory performance will be determined and by whom. Initial performance reviews usually focus on demonstration that employees are able to successfully carry out the main functions identified in the job description that they were hired to fill and that they have adapted to the organization more generally.

The organization should retain the right to extend the introductory period for up to three months. This covers the situation when employees have not fully achieved the expected competency levels to fulfill their job, but the employer wishes to give the employees additional time to demonstrate they can do the job.

Policy

"Introductory period" refers to a period of up to three months of employment for a newly hired employee. At the end of the introductory period, an employee who has demonstrated satisfactory competence in fulfilling the functions in the position and integration into the organization may become regular full-time or part-time employee. Other factors in the organization such as availability of funds, the continued need for the position, and expectations for continuing satisfactory work performance in the position may influence the appointment as a regular employee. Termination can occur at any time during and after the introductory period if the employee's performance consistently fails to meet minimum performance standards.

After completing the introductory period, the prospective full-time staff member is eligible for selected, nonmandatory benefits available to regular employees of the organization.

A noncompensation-related performance evaluation by the staff person's supervisor will determine whether the introductory period has been completed satisfactorily. Current employees who are promoted or placed in a new job are subject to these policies regarding introductory period except that they will retain their regular employee benefits.

ORIENTATION

Rationale

It is costly to recruit, select, and place new employees. A well-thought-out and effective orientation program is an important step in achieving a good employee/employer relationship. The orientation should help employees understand the nonprofit's historical development, vision, mission, values, long-range goals, and annual plan, including and especially the plan for the area in which they are starting work. They also should learn about the current organization structure, including the role of the membership if members are a part of the governance of the organization, the board of directors and its committees, and the staff. Employees need to understand the programs and services offered and to whom. Most of all, they need to know how what they do contributes to the overall success of the nonprofit and its mission. The person's supervisor will want to review the job description and the goals or performance standards for the new employee's position with the new employee. The expectations for successful completion of the introductory period should be made explicit along with the means by which performance will be evaluated. Note that this process is appropriate to existing employees taking new positions as well as those employees recruited from outside the organization.

This is also the time when the new employee is made to feel welcome and the socialization process begins. The person's supervisor may provide a tour and introductions or assign the responsibility to another staff person. When there is a human resource department, it also may be involved in orientation. Clear responsibility should be assigned to the appropriate management staff in regard to explaining compensation and benefits and ensuring that the organization is in compliance with the required enrollments and new employee procedures.

A checklist of what is covered in the orientation that the new employee signs is a good way to ensure the orientation is fully completed. The new employee's signature on the checklist protects the organization should employment issues arise and the employee states he or she was not properly informed about items during the orientation.

LETTER OF HIRE

Rationale

The letter of hire should explain the current conditions of employment. It should state the specific position the candidate is hired to fill, the name of the nonprofit, the starting date, the beginning pay, and the offer of the position. Candidates should sign one copy and return it to the employer and keep a copy for themselves.

ALCOHOL AND DRUG TESTING

Rationale

Nonprofits may wish to adopt a policy that states their right to test newly hired staff and current employees for drugs and alcohol. The policy should state the circumstances when this testing will be done.

Applicants will be tested when they are offered employment. Some employers actually post a notice that applicants can plainly see, notifying them that they will be subject to testing and telling them not to apply if they are drug users. Current staff members can be tested at random, when they are involved in an accident on the job in which a personal injury occurs, or if there is reasonable suspicion of their being under the influence of drugs or alcohol. Reasonable suspicion could include aggressive or disoriented behavior, personality changes, odor of alcohol or marijuana, and the like.

The policy can include statements that those staff members who refuse to be tested can face immediate dismissal and that current staff members who fail the test will be referred to a chemical dependency treatment program.

If the nonprofit is a state or federal government contractor, it is covered by the Federal Drug-Free Workplace Act. Management should be familiar with the act and the rules and regulations on administering it.

PHYSICAL EXAMINATION

Rationale

Under the Americans with Disabilities Act, job applicants may not be required to pass a prehiring physical examination. However, persons who have been offered a job can be asked to complete an examination before they start work to determine how well they can perform the essential functions of the job.

Federal, state, or local laws; statute regulations; or licensing authorities also may require that certain classifications of staff undergo periodic physicals.

EMPLOYEE BACKGROUND CHECKS

Rationale

A good job application form will ask the applicant to list two or three professional or personal references, and the nonprofit should contact these individuals. The nonprofit can do so itself; if it uses a third party, the Fair Credit Reporting Act comes into play.

CRIMINAL BACKGROUND CHECKS

Rationale

Using the nonprofit's mission as a gauge, an organization can determine the amount of risk it wishes to accept in terms of its hiring policies and criminal background checks. For example, if the service recipients are children or other vulnerable populations, the focus point of the background checks might be for a record of crimes against such persons. The nonprofit has the responsibility to protect its service recipients from harm.

Background checks are part of the applicant screening process. The screening process should state what offenses are relevant, other factors that may be considered, and how the rights of the applicant will be preserved. Relevant offenses are related to the position the person may fill. State and local laws must be taken into account. Other factors the nonprofit may wish to include when considering if the offense will influence further consideration of the applicant are:

- Age of individual at the time the offense occurred
- Societal conditions as they relate to the conduct
- Whether the behavior forms part of a pattern or was a one-time occurrence
- What steps the individual took to become rehabilitated

Applicants should be given the right to challenge the accuracy of the information received by the nonprofit. They must take the lead in resolving inaccuracies. The nonprofit must safeguard the privacy of the individual and protect against misuse of the background records. For more information, check with the Nonprofit Risk Management Center (www.nonprofitrisk.com).

TERMINATION

RESIGNATION

Rationale

Staff members decide to terminate their employment for various personal and professional reasons. When they do, their resignation should be accepted graciously and with respect for their interests. However, they can be expected to follow the notice policies as determined in the personnel policies. The policies should state how much notice is required and how the resignation is to be submitted and to whom. It is wise to ask for written notice. Higher-level positions in the organization may be required to give longer notice. Notice periods of a month are not uncommon, as replacements may be harder to recruit and the organization may be more vulnerable if high-level positions are vacant for a longer time. Two weeks' notice is usual for exempt positions.

In cases when departing employees might be disgruntled and create a morale or security risk, they may be asked to stop coming to work once they turn in their resignation notice. An exit interview provides an opportunity to learn about the experience of employees. Such information can be useful in improving working conditions or preserving and building on conditions that are highly valued.

RELEASING JOB REFERENCES

Rationale

Increasingly, organizations provide only confirmation of the position the person held and the period of employment. A definite procedure should be set in place for answering job reference inquiries. One person often is designated to respond to these inquiries, so the responses are controlled. The person is usually the executive director or the human resource manager. Some attorneys recommend that departing employees sign a waiver of liability (see Exhibit 3.2) before they leave the nonprofit.

Policy

EXHIBIT 3.2   REFERENCE RELEASE WAIVER

I authorize this nonprofit to furnish any future employers with whom I seek employment with whatever information they may desire regarding my employment here, including my reason(s) for leaving. I am signing this waiver voluntarily, and request that this nonprofit respond to all reference inquiries with full and complete information.

Because this reference is an important part of my application for my future employment, I therefore waive and release this nonprofit from any and all claims or causes of action in law or equity, including, but not limited to, defamation of character or invasion of privacy, which might arise from responding to a reference check.

_____   _____

Staff Member Signature   Date

_____   _____

Supervisor Signature   Date

DISMISSAL

Rationale

Dismissal may come as the final step in a progressive disciplinary policy, or as the justification in firing a staff person who commits a serious offense involving the nonprofit. It also may come due to organization circumstances not related to the staff person. In each instance, the personnel policies will be the backbone of the action taken. Remember, as an at-will employer, a staff person can be terminated at any time, for any reason. If your state does not recognize at-will statements, the organization must prove just cause for dismissal.

Proving just cause requires careful documentation of the steps leading to the dismissal to show that the staff person was dismissed for valid reasons. Careful documentation of action concerning an employee, job performance, and any other incidents involving the employment status of the staff member is appropriate regardless of state law. The expectation for such documentation along with procedures to accomplish it should be communicated to all supervisors, who should be required to demonstrate their compliance with these procedures. Confidential personnel files should be kept that include all relevant employment history.

In the case of serious misconduct on the job, dismissal action may be immediate. The organization's personnel policies should include a list of behaviors warranting immediate dismissal.

Policy

Dismissal may come from the need for the organization to alter its workforce, which may be due to financial considerations, reorganization, or other organizational issues. Or it may occur when an employee has failed to meet employment expectations or has committed a serious offense. Prior to dismissal, the executive director should review and approve the decision to dismiss the employee. Explanations to the employee about the reasons for dismissal should be determined and communicated to the employee through official channels. Dismissal notices should include the date employment ends, whether the employee is expected to work during the notice period, and general statements about the cause for dismissal, for example, due to reorganization of the nonprofit that resulted in the employees position being eliminated. It is not appropriate to go into details about the cause of dismissal in the dismissal letter.

Some offenses warrant immediate dismissal. These offenses include but are not limited to:

- Theft including, but not limited to, the removal of company property or the property of another staff member from company premises without prior authorization.

- Drugs/alcohol possession, use, sale, purchase, or distribution on non-profit property of alcohol or any illegally possessed drugs. Also, reporting to work after having ingested alcohol or illegal drugs or illegally possessed drugs, in a condition that adversely affects the staff member's ability to safely and effectively perform his or her job functions, or that would imperil the safety of other staff members.

- Falsifying or altering company records.

- Sabotaging or willfully damaging nonprofit equipment or the property of others.

- Walking off the job without supervisory permission.

- Insubordination involving, but not limited to, defaming, assaulting, or threatening to assault a supervisor and refusing to carry out the order of a supervisor where personal safety is not a problem.

- Fighting or provoking a fight on company premises.

- Absence for three consecutive working days without notice to the non-profit, in which event the offending staff member will be deemed to have quit voluntarily.

- Carrying concealed weapons on nonprofit property.

CHAPTER 4

Compensation Policies

This chapter covers policies related to administration of various forms of compensation including salaries, benefits, and innovative compensation.

ESTABLISHING A COMPENSATION POLICY (IRS INTERMEDIATE SANCTIONS AND THEIR EFFECT ON COMPENSATION POLICIES)

Rationale

When a nonprofit corporation is granted tax-exempt status under IRS Section 501(c)(3) of the Internal Revenue Code, the corporation obtains a dual benefit: The corporation does not have to pay income taxes, and individuals who contribute to a nonprofit with this status can deduct contributions from their income tax. In return for this status, charitable organizations must ensure that no part of the net earnings inures to provide an advantaged benefit to any individual or shareholder. Inurement most likely concerns persons associated closely with the organization, such as officers, directors, founders, top management, and their families. Excessive benefit may be through salaries or other forms of compensation.

The board of directors is responsible for the nonprofit's compensation policies and their implementation. Boards are required to ensure that the organization's resources are used prudently and carefully to accomplish the mission of the organization under their duty of care legal standard. They must assure that private inurement and excessive benefit to an individual does not occur.

In the early 1990s, concerns grew about excessive compensation in non-profits due, at least in part, to widely publized excessive compensation scandals, such as the excessive compensation of executive William Aramony of the United Way of America and other UWA senior officers. In 1996 Congress enacted Section 4958 of the IRS Code, which has become known as the Intermediate Sanctions provision. On January 10, 2001 the Treasury issued temporary regulations, which are effective for a three-year period and expire January 9, 2004, when final regulations are expected. The Intermediate Sanctions provisions apply to transactions occurring on or after September 14, 1995.

Prior to the passage of the Intermediate Sanctions, the IRS has had only one penalty available with which to sanction a nonprofit corporation found to be in violation of its 501(c)(3) exemption: revocation of that charity's tax-exempt status. Revocation of a charity's 501(c)(3) exemption is a drastic measure that could cause great harm to the constituency served by the charity and was seldom used by the IRS. Under the Intermediate Sanctions Act, the IRS has a broad range of options, short of revocation, for penalizing 501(c)(3)(4) public charities, their staffs, and their volunteers for using organizational assets for inappropriate personal gain and benefit. The IRS may impose penalty excise taxes on disqualified persons and managers of organizations that engage in an excess benefit transaction. An excess benefit transaction is any transaction in which an economic benefit is provided by the exempt organization directly or indirectly to or for the use of any disqualified person if the value of the economic benefit provided exceeds the value of the consideration (including the performance of services) provided in return. A disqualified person is defined as a person (including not only a natural person but also a trust, estate, partnership, corporation, or other entity) in a position to exercise substantial influence over the affairs of the exempt organization, specifically including directors and officers thereof. A disqualified person also includes certain members of the family of a disqualified person or an entity in which a disqualified person holds more than 35 percent of the ownership or beneficial interests. Disqualified persons also include any other person who has substantial influence over the exempt organization, such as a substantial contributor. An organization manager includes any director, trustee, or officer of the exempt organization, or any individual having powers or responsibilities similar to those of directors, trustees, or officers.

The Proposed Regulations under Code 4958, issued on July 30, 1998, provide a "rebuttable presumption" that compensation paid is reasonable, and consideration paid for property transfers is the fair market value, if the decision-making process with respect to the transaction follows certain prescribed procedures. However, even if the presumption were not specifically provided in the Proposed Regulations, the prescribed procedures represent "best practices" that should be followed when entering into any compensation arrangement or property transfer involving a disqualified person. The IRS states that payments under a compensation arrangement are presumed reasonable and transfer of property is presumed to be at fair market value, if these three conditions are met:

1. An authorized body of the organization approves the transaction (or the entity it controls). It is composed of individuals who do not have a conflict of interest concerning the transaction.

2. Prior to making its determination, the authorized body obtained and relied on appropriate data as to comparability. There is a special safe harbor for small organizations, if the organization has gross receipts of less than $1 million; appropriate comparable data includes data on compensation paid by three comparable organizations in the same or similar communities for similar services.

3. The authorized body adequately documents the basis for its determination concurrently with making that decision. The documentation should include:

   a. The terms of the approved transaction and the date approved.

   b. The members of the authorized body who were present during debate on the transaction that was approved and who voted on it.

   c. The comparability data obtained and relied on by the authorized body and how the data was obtained.

   d. Any interests by a member of the authorized body having a conflict of interest.

   e. Documentation of the basis for the determination before the later of the meeting of the authorized body or 60 days after the final actions of the authorized body are taken, and approval of records, as reasonable, accurate, and complete, within a reasonable time thereafter.

For further information, go to www.irs.gov/charities/index.htm and search for "intermediate sanctions."

Exhibit 4.1 is a checklist for development of a compensation policy that a nonprofit can use. It incorporates the requirements of the Intermediate Sanctions compliance and good governance and management practices.

Policy

EXHIBIT 4.1   CHECKLIST FOR DEVELOPMENT OF A COMPENSATION PROGRAM

Recruiting a Compensation Committee

☐ A work unit of the board of directors, hereafter referred to as the compensation committee, will be responsible for the development of the compensation policies. The work unit can be a committee, a subcommittee, or in the case of a small board, the board itself. The size of the work unit can vary depending on the structure of the organization; the typical size might be three to five directors.

☐ The board should develop and authorize, according to the bylaws or traditional means, a written compensation committee charge, including the responsibilities and procedures.

☐ The members of the compensation committee should have the necessary knowledge to accomplish the work. Examples of appropriate professionals with relevant background include human resource specialists, accountants, attorneys, management specialists, etc.

☐ Members of the committee may not have financial or other significant social or personal relationships with the executive or other staff. The executive should see that the committee has adequate staff support but will not function as a member of the committee.

Preparation for Developing the Organization's Compensation Policies

Gather internal background information, including:

☐ Organization history and culture.

☐ Vision statement, mission statement, values, long-range goals, and annual plan.

☐ Organization chart.

☐ Current job descriptions, number of people in each position, employee tenure, and turnover information.

☐ Summarized employee demographics, tenure, turnover rate, employee surveys, exit interview summary information.

EXHIBIT 4.1   CONTINUED

☐ Personnel polices.

☐ Previous compensation studies and policies including cash and innovative compensation.

☐ Input from board, executive managers, and supervisors regarding workforce concerns and preferences related to compensation policies.

☐ Current employee motivations and those of prospective employee markets.

☐ Need for consultant has been evaluated and consultant obtained if appropriate.

Gather external background information, including:

☐ Appropriate workforce and market pricing data.

☐ Innovative compensation practices reviewed to determine which ones are of interest.

Identify desired outcomes:

☐ Identify outcomes to be achieved from the compensation policies and obtain agreement from organization leadership.

☐ Evaluate need for additional data and obtain data as appropriate.

Update/Alter Current Policies and Practices to Reflect Desired Outcomes

☐ Review the organization chart, job descriptions, and relevant sections of the personnel policies and update them to reflect current reality and future desired directions.

☐ Revise or establish basic wage scales and benefits.

☐ Review equity in current compensation within the organization and identify and address any corrective actions.

☐ Obtain employee reaction to prospective innovative compensation.

☐ Obtain additional advice or information to allow for choices to be made about which, if any, innovative practices fit the compensation policy outcomes.

☐ Make decisions on the innovative compensation practices that will be included in the new compensation policies.

Implement New Policies

☐ Develop an integrated compensation plan.

☐ The board has approved the plan, and monitoring and evaluation mechanisms are in place.

☐ The plan has been communicated to employees.

Source: Adapted from a form first published in *Nonprofit Compensation and Benefits Practices*, by Carol L. Barbeito and Jack P. Bowman (New York: John Wiley & Sons, Inc., 1998), 15.

Employment Status

Rationale

Staff members may be classified as full-time regular, part-time regular, or temporary. These classifications usually are defined in personnel policies, and policies, compensation, and benefits may vary according to the employee classification.

Policy

Staff categories as established by this nonprofit organization are:

- *Regular Full-time Employees*: Individuals employed to work a full basic workweek of 35 or 40 hours, of unlimited employment duration.

- *Regular Part-time Employees*: Individuals employed to work a basic workweek for a set number of hours that are fewer than 35, of unlimited employment duration.

- *Temporary Workers*: Individuals employed for a specified, limited period of time, either on a full- or part-time basis.

Compensatory Time and Overtime

Exempt and Nonexempt Staff Classifications

Rationale

The United States Department of Labor administers the Fair Labor Standards Act. The act delineates exempt and nonexempt employee definitions and when employers must pay nonexempt employees for overtime work. The chart in Exhibit 4.2 can serve as a guideline when deciding when the law requires overtime pay for staff members. If a staff member fulfills all the requirements in any one of the three categories listed in the exhibit, the staff member would be considered exempt and overtime pay is not required. Note: In 2003 Congress was considering revisions to the definition of exempt and nonexempt employees and the policies regarding overtime compensation so it is wise to follow these pending changes closely.

EXHIBIT 4.2	GUIDE TO OVERTIME PAY ISSUES		
Requirements	**Executive Category**	**Administrative Category**	**Professional Category**
Primary duties: (generally take up 50% of staff time)	The executive staff manages the nonprofit or a customarily recognized department or subdivision.	The administrative staff is responsible for office or nonmanual work related to management policies or general business operations *or* is responsible for work that is directly related to academic instruction or training carried on in the administration of a school system or educational establishment.	The professional staff performs work requiring advanced knowledge in a field of science or learning, usually obtained by a prolonged course of specialized instruction and study *or* works as a certified or recognized teacher in the workplace.
Other duties:	No additional duties are required.	The staff regularly assists an executive or administrative employee *or* performs work under only general supervision along specialized or technical lines requiring special training, knowledge, or experience *or* works on special assignments under only general supervision. **NOTE:** Academic administrative personnel perform work directly in the field of education.	The staff must do work that is mostly intellectual and varied rather than simply routine or mechanical duties.

(continues)

EXHIBIT 4.2   CONTINUED

Requirements	Executive Category	Administrative Category	Professional Category
Supervision of other staff members:	The staff member must customarily and regularly supervise the equivalent of two full-time staff members.	No specific requirement.	No specific requirement.
Authority:	The executive staff must have authority to fire or recommend hiring and firing or must be a staff member whose recommendation on actions affecting other staff members is given particular weight.	No authority required.	No authority required.
Discretion used in performing duties:	The executive staff must customarily and regularly use discretionary powers.	The administrative staff must customarily and regularly use discretion and independent judgment, rather than simply using skills and following procedures, and must have the authority to make important decisions.	The professional staff must consistently use discretion and judgment.
Amount of time performing nonexempt work:	The executive staff member spends no more than 20% of time performing activities not directly and closely related to managerial duties.	The administrative staff member spends no more than 20% of time performing duties not directly and closely related to administrative duties.	The professional member spends no more than 20% of time performing duties not essentially a part of professional duties.

EXHIBIT 4.2   CONTINUED

Requirements	Executive Category	Administrative Category	Professional Category
Minimum salaries paid: (not in Puerto Rico, Virgin Islands, or American Samoa; exclusive of board, lodging, and other facilities)	Staff member earns at least $155 a week.	Staff member earns at least $155 a week.	Staff member earns at least $170 a week. **Exceptions:** Licensed legal and medical practitioners, holders of academic medical degrees and engaged in internship or residency, teachers in schools or educational institutions.

Source: Compiled from information found in "Executive, Administrative, Professional and Outside Sales Exemptions Under the Fair Labor Standards Act," U.S. Department of Labor, Employment Standards Administration, Wage and Hour Division, WH Publication 1363. For a free copy of this bulletin, contact a local Wage and Hour office listed in the phone book under Department of Labor, or call (866) 487-9243. Information on this chart is a guide for overtime pay issues only. It should not be used for issues like providing break time or other benefits.[1]

COMPENSATORY TIME FOR EXEMPT EMPLOYEES

Rationale

Nonexempt employees must be paid overtime if they work more than 40 hours in a week, according to the Wage Hour Act. The nonprofit organization can determine if and how it wants to compensate exempt employees. They can be paid overtime, given compensatory time, given extra annual leave, or given no extra compensation. Exempt staff morale is a consideration if overtime for exempt staff is extensive with no reward system attached to the extra time. Other concerns may be employees' health and the avoidance of unrealistic expectations of staff that ultimately can produce negative results for the employee and the organization. Also, having a clear policy about exempt staff overtime that is applied evenly throughout the exempt staff workforce helps avoid misunderstandings.

OVERTIME APPROVAL FOR NONEXEMPT EMPLOYEES

Rationale

Uncontrolled overtime can be expensive for a nonprofit. Therefore, it is recommended that nonexempt employees request and receive approval in advance of working overtime. Use of an overtime request form, which includes the employee's name, job title, dates of overtime work, and the estimated number of hours to be worked, works well. The employee's supervisor should have approval power. The executive director should monitor overtime use through financial or other reports.

Policy

All nonexempt staff members—for example, those whose jobs are classified as being subject to the Fair Labor Standards Act's overtime pay provisions—are eligible for overtime compensation.

All overtime, however, must be approved by the staff member's immediate supervisor in written form (see Exhibit 4.3) and submitted to the executive director prior to working the overtime hours.

EXHIBIT 4.3   APPROVAL FOR PAID OVERTIME FOR NONEXEMPT EMPLOYEES

I authorize _____ to work the estimated overtime as specified below and that time and half wages will be paid for actual hours worked overtime. This form is to be submitted with the employee's time sheet for the work period in which the overtime hours occurred.

Date(s) of Projected Overtime: _____   Estimated time to be worked: _____

_____   _____
Employee Signature   Date

_____   _____
Supervisor Signature   Date

TEMPORARY LABORERS

Rationale

There has been a strong trend over the last several years for employers to utilize temporary labor rather than hire full- or part-time regular employees. Temporary labor works well when the work to be done is seasonal, time-limited, of a specialized nature that the organization cannot otherwise afford, when the budget or situation of the organization makes it unwise to commit to a new employee, and no doubt many other circumstances. The plus side of this arrangement for the organization is that it can obtain the help needed without offering ongoing employment subject to accompanying compensation policies including benefits, paid leave, and compliance with laws that pertain to employees.

Temporary employees often do not receive any benefits. Specific rules about payment of legally mandated benefits relate to the amount of time worked in both hours and length of service. Outsourcing, in which work is contracted to other firms or individuals and they are paid according to the contract with the nonprofit for the service provided, is another arrangement for getting work done without hiring employees. Further, independent contractors agree to complete work specific for the organization and are responsible for their own benefits and legal compliance. Nonprofits will want to evaluate if any of these arrangements suit their needs. Legal advice is important to obtain and follow when establishing policies related to temporary workers and independent contractors.

INDEPENDENT CONTRACTORS

Rationale

Independent contractors are not considered employees and therefore are not covered by mandatory benefits. These are contractors who perform service for an organization. The trick is to determine if workers are truly "independent." The IRS uses common law factors including:

- Can the contractor be fired or quit without contractual liability?
- Is the contractor paid by the hour, week, or month rather than by the job?
- Is the contractor reimbursed for business and travel expenses?

- Does the contractor perform the task in person, on company property, and during set hours?
- Does the organization provide the contractor with tools or equipment?

If the answers are yes, the independence of the contractor is questionable and mandated benefits most likely should be paid. The National Labor Relations Board uses common law, right to control, and degree of investment of the worker and the opportunity for entrepreneurial profit and loss. The Department of Labor uses an economic reality test as to whether the worker is economically dependent on the employer to whom service is provided along with right to control.

Nonprofits should use these factors and take care not to use independent contractor status as a way to avoid paying someone who is truly an employee mandated benefits.

MERIT SALARY INCREASES

Rationale

There is a strong trend among nonprofit organizations to base salary increases on merit as a motivational tool that rewards top performers and does not reward below-average performance. Merit increases are based on employee performance against job duties, goals, and other performance targets that are pre-identified at the start of the employment period, usually one year. They are not automatic and do not support an entitlement mentality among employees. Raises must be earned through average to superior performance. However, note that absence of job descriptions, clear goals and objectives the employee is contributing to or responsible for, and a functioning performance appraisal system will make successful implementation of merit-based salary increases difficult and less effective. Employees should be fully informed about how and when they will receive salary increases and what types of increases are available.

Cost-of-living increases are usually organization-wide and reflect adjustments for inflation. A government model is for step increases based on completion of each year of service. This type of increase is increasingly out of favor as it rewards staying in place in a job rather than job performance, and poor and excellent performers are not differentiated between when raises are awarded. Governments are moving slowly toward performance-based pay. Many organizations combine cost-of-living salary adjustment when inflation warrants it with performance-based salary increases.

Policy

A salary range has been established for each regular staff position. All salaries are gross salaries and are subject to mandatory and voluntary deductions.

- Salary increases are based on performance of job functions, goals, and objectives and other employee performance measures as identified in the employee's performance appraisal, which is done at least annually. For new employees or for employees in new positions or those with performance concerns, appraisals may be done more often.
- The board of directors approves salary ranges for all positions. Periodically, the board will authorize a review of the salary ranges to ensure they remain competitive and appropriate to the human resource philosophies of the organization.
- Cost-of-living adjustments are different from merit increases and usually are reflective of an across-the-board adjustment in wage scales in response to external economic conditions. The board of directors authorizes such adjustments.

ADVANCE PAY

Rationale

An advance pay policy specifically states if and when salary or wages will be advanced. The advance generally is recommended to the executive director on the approval of the employee's supervisor. The request and approval should be made in writing. Pay advances should be limited to emergency situations, and what constitutes an emergency should be defined. The policy should cover other conditions for granting advance pay, such as having sufficient accrued vacation time to cover the advance and being an employee in good standing.

Policy

Pay advances are granted at the nonprofit's discretion and only in cases that constitute an emergency, such as a home fire or need to travel due to family catastrophe.

Pay advances are drawn against earned wages. The supervisor will recommend the staff member's request made in writing for approval by the executive director.

TIME SHEETS

Rationale

Use of time sheets for all employees accomplishes several things. First, it verifies days or hours worked, sick leave or other leave taken, and use of vacation time. Time sheets should be completed and filed with the supervisor for each pay period on a timely basis, and issuance of paychecks should be dependent on the receipt of the time sheet approved by the supervisor. Leave request forms should be attached. Another benefit of time sheets is that they also may provide an important basis for functional accounting allocations, which the nonprofit uses to determine how much time is spent on program versus management in general and fund raising and can aid in tracking restricted grant expenditures. Employees are provided with codes, and the time sheet includes codes indicating what functions the employee was performing during each time segment. This coding also can provide documentation of time spent on restricted grants, which makes grant reporting easier.

TEMPORARY SALARY ADJUSTMENTS

Rationale

On occasion, an employee may be asked to temporarily take on the duties of another employee, which adds responsibility and increases workload. Consideration should be given as to whether the employee assuming the extra duties should receive additional compensation during this period. For example, during the short-term illness of another employee, everyone may need to pitch in and take on extra work. When the additional responsibilities are to be assumed for an extended period, it is appropriate to make a temporary salary adjustment.

If a temporary salary adjustment is done, be sure to specify the period for the adjustment in writing. When the employee returns to performing only their usual duties, rescind the salary adjustment in writing. In addition to compensation adjustments, special recognition commending the staff person who took on the extra duties provides another way to reward cooperation and serves as a good example to other employees. Ideas for such recognition include a thank-you letter from the executive director or other supervisors, public acknowledgment in staff meetings, and notes in personnel files.

TRAVEL ADVANCES

Rationale

Organizations that require employees to travel to conduct their business may need to provide travel advances to help them cover their expenses. Sometimes a company credit card can be provided, but often the employee is allowed to draw a cash advance, which may or may not be in addition to having access to a credit card. Employees should be informed when hired how to apply for travel advances, the procedures for accounting for expenditures, and for the return of unused portions of the advance.

Policy

In anticipation of travel expenses, employees may qualify to draw an advance that will cover expenses, which would pose a hardship for employees to cover on their own before reimbursement by the organization.

Supervisors must submit employees' requests for advance payment (see Exhibit 4.4) for approval by the executive director 10 days prior to the beginning of travel. Expenses to be reimbursed are defined by other travel policies. Any unused portion of the advance must be returned when the receipts of expenses are filed within 5 days of completion of travel.

EXHIBIT 4.4   TRAVEL ADVANCE REQUEST

Employee Name:_____   Title: _____

Purpose of Travel:_____

Departure Date: _____   Return Date: _____

Traveling to: _____

Amount of Travel Advance: $ _____

Travel Advance Recommended by Supervisor: _____

Approval by Executive Director: _____

FINAL PAY

Rationale

When staff persons leave the employment of a nonprofit organization, for whatever reason, they are entitled to any money due them. Any failure to compensate them properly and promptly can create problems.

In most states, staff members are legally eligible to be paid for all time worked plus accrued vacation time. State law should be checked to ensure compliance. The nonprofit may choose to have more generous policies regarding calculation of final pay than the law requires. Policies in regard to leave benefits should be part of the personnel policies approved by the board of directors. Conversion rights of leave benefits to cash or other benefit types should be explicit.

Nonprofits will want property issued to the departing staff member returned. A proactive approach to this is wise. Ask all employees to sign a form that lists the items when they are issued to them, which states that, if the items are not returned, their final pay will be reduced in an amount equal to the value of all nonreturned items (see Exhibit 4.5). In most states it is illegal to require employees to sign such a form unless they consent.

Staff members who leave the nonprofit are also entitled, for 18 months following termination, to continued health insurance coverage under the employer's group plan, at their own expense. Federal law requires that the organization explain this to each employee. To be on the safe side, a nonprofit should make communicating this information one of the steps in the final pay policy. Also, employees should sign a form that verifies that this benefit has been explained and indicates in writing whether they have accepted the Consolidated Omnibus Budget Reconciliation Act of 1986 (COBRA) benefit or rejected it.

Policy

EXHIBIT 4.5 FINAL PAY AGREEMENT

I understand that upon my separation from this nonprofit, I am responsible for returning any nonprofit equipment or property issued to me, including keys. If I fail to return any such items, I agree that the nonprofit may withhold from my final paycheck an amount equal to the value of the nonreturned items.

The following items have been issued to

_____

(*Print name*)

Item	Date of Issue	Date of Return
_____	_____	_____
_____	_____	_____
_____	_____	_____
_____	_____	_____
_____	_____	_____
_____	_____	_____
_____	_____	_____
_____	_____	_____

_____   _____

Staff Member's Signature   Date

_____

SALARIES

SALARY RANGES

Rationale

Salary ranges should be established for each staff position. Factors that will influence the ranges include: a job description that outlines duties, responsibilities, and qualifications; comparable salaries paid by like organizations; geographic location and its influence on cost of living; difficulty in recruiting and retaining employees with the necessary qualifications; economic factors such as rate of inflation; the human resource philosophy of the organization; and the budget. The ranges are not for specific employees but rather should be set for the job positions; but those people who establish the ranges will want to know how current employees' salaries fit into the ranges.

Relationships between ranges for all jobs are a factor to consider and it is a good idea to review all salary ranges periodically. In general, the ranges will be broader for higher-level positions than for lower-level positions. A rationale for this is that turnover of top management and professional positions has more negative impact on the organization, and broader ranges provide incentives for such employees to stay with the organization longer. Ranges will define the starting salary for new employees who meet job qualifications; they also define the highest salary deemed appropriate for that position. Some ranges will state the minimum, middle, and maximum of the ranges.

SEVERANCE PAY

Rationale

Personnel policies generally state a notice requirement when employees resign or are terminated. During the notice period, employees are paid their normal salary and benefits continue. The nonprofit may wish to enrich this benefit if an employee is in good standing and is leaving due to the circumstances of the organization, such as merger, layoffs, or reorganization. The formula for severance pay is up to the nonprofit. One factor that might be considered in determining the benefit is length of employment. Issuing the severance pay in a lump sum eliminates confusion about when employment actually terminated, which is useful if the employee files for unemployment and helps in determining how the termination affects benefits.

BENEFITS

BENEFIT PHILOSOPHY STATEMENT

Rationale

Benefits are an important part of the total compensation package for employees. Therefore, it is important for the nonprofit organization to spend some time defining in a philosophy statement how it views benefits and what it is trying to achieve through personnel benefits. This statement is used to communicate to prospective and current employees and is a tool in recruitment and retention of employees. Further, it provides guidance to administrators in selection and implementation of the benefits program. Such a statement usually is developed through staff input to a human resource committee of the board and adopted by the board of directors. The executive director is then responsible for managing the benefits program in concert with the philosophy statement.

Policy

The University of Denver recognizes that to fulfill its mission it requires a diverse group of highly qualified employees-educators, researchers, administrators, and support staff. The University maintains a comprehensive and competitive benefits program to help ensure it attracts and retains the people needed to carry out its mission.

Therefore, the University of Denver will deliver an employee benefits program that:

- Provides a "safety net" of basic benefits protection against the financial impact of catastrophic life events.
- Recognizes benefits are an important element of total compensation from the University.
- Provides flexibility over the design and cost of benefits in order to deliver the highest quality and value at a reasonable cost for both the individual and the University.
- Reflects principles of sound financial management, fiscal responsibility, regulatory compliance, and administrative efficiency at all times.
- Is communicated effectively to promote full understanding and value of the benefits program.
- Provides personal service to individual participants to ensure they receive full benefits from available programs.
- Is dynamic and innovative, changing as necessary to meet the changing needs and balancing of work-life issues of both employees and the University.
- Utilizes central policy development to promote fairness and equity judiciously, while supporting the University's value of decentralization, flexibility and responsiveness.
- Encourages enrollment in cost-effective plans.

- Assists the University to compete successfully for human resources in all areas of activity.

- Promotes consistency in availability of benefits coverage among employee groups.

- Offers opportunities to enhance the basic benefit package, so that employees can address their particular benefit needs.[2]

MANDATORY BENEFITS

Rationale

All employers are required to contribute to Social Security, unemployment compensation, and workers' compensation benefits.

- Social Security provides retirement, disability, death, survivor, and Medicare benefits for those beyond age 65.

- Unemployment compensation provides temporary and partial wages to employees who have been laid off through no fault of their own for a period of time until they have new employment. State laws vary.

- Workingman's Compensation is an employer-financed insurance program that provides compensation to employees who are unable to work because of job-related injury or illness. State laws may vary.

Detailed information on each mandated benefit can be found at

a. www.ssa.gov/pubs/10029.html for Social Security

b. www.coworkforce.com/uib for example of state on Unemployment Compensation

c. www.doli.state.mn.us/workcomp for a state example of Workingman's Compensation

INSURANCE BENEFITS

Rationale

The type of benefits the organization offers, including leave policies, usually are defined in the personnel policies. However, because the nonprofit may need to change insurance providers and plans, the specifics of insurance plans should not be in the policies. Rather, staff members should be provided with a summary of all the insurance plans, and the insurance providers should provide suitable handouts for employees, explaining each plan in everyday terms. Organization procedures regarding insurance benefit programs also should be provided in writing to all employees. The organization will want to make clear to whom the benefits are available and when an employee can begin receiving the benefits.

An employee who declines a group insurance plan should be asked to sign a waiver of benefits form (see Exhibit 4.6 on pages 81–82). Nonprofits should watch for legislation or changes to rules and regulations that might affect insurance benefit coverage or administration.

The Health Insurance Portability and Accountability Act (HIPAA) took effect July 1, 1997. This law ensures that most persons who change jobs will receive continuous health insurance without regard to many preexisting health conditions. Many nonprofits are affected by HIPAA's certification requirements.

All nonprofits with group health plans that include two or more participants who are current employees are subject to HIPAA's provisions. This applies to self-insured group health plans as well as plans provided by an insurance carrier.

HIPAA allows staff members who have been covered by health insurance for 12 continuous months to switch employers and employer insurance plans without having to undergo waiting periods for preexisting conditions.

The law affects staff persons who leave a job and new enrollees in health insurance plans.

The U.S. Department of Labor cites these provisions of the law that nonprofits need to be aware of:

- HIPAA restricts the circumstances under which a plan can exclude participants for preexisting conditions.

- Under HIPAA, a health insurance plan must state if there is a preexisting condition exclusion and can exclude people from coverage only after they have been notified. The limitation on preexisting conditions is 12 months (18 months if the covered person is a "late enrollee" in the plan).

If a person can show continuous coverage on a previous plan with no more than a 63-day break in coverage, the exclusion period must be reduced by the number of days of creditable coverage. Creditable coverage includes a group health plan, health maintenance organization (HMO), individual health insurance policy, Consolidated Omnibus Budget Reconciliation Act (COBRA), Medicaid, or Medicare.

Nonprofits should review health insurance plans with the provider to determine how preexisting conditions provisions are handled.

1. *Certification of coverage.* The nonprofit organization will be expected to provide certification within "a reasonable time after coverage ceases." The suggested certification should include:

   • Name of the group health plan

   • The name and identification number of the participant

   • The name(s) of dependents covered by the policy

   • Name, address, and telephone number of the plan administrator or insurance company responsible for providing this certificate

   • Dates coverage began and ended, as well as dates of waiting periods (if applicable)

   The health insurance carrier that manages the plan may be willing to provide the certification. According to the Department of Labor's guidance, the organization will be responsible for providing certification to those staff members who lost coverage or began COBRA coverage between October 1, 1996 and May 31, 1997. These staff members will need this certification when they apply for health coverage on an independent plan or through another group plan.

   Certification for dependents covered on a policy may be made by noting the type of coverage on the staff person's certificate (family, employee plus spouse) and must make reasonable efforts to include the names of dependents on coverage certificates.

2. *Disclosure requirements.* HIPAA requires group health plans to improve their summary plan descriptions in four ways:

   1. Notify plan participants and beneficiaries of reductions in benefits or services, or increases in deductibles or copayments within 60 days of adoption.

   2. Disclose the role of insurance companies, HMOs, or other providers with respect to the health plan, including information about contracts or policies guaranteeing benefits and the nature of administrative services provided.

3. Inform staff members and dependents about which Department of Labor office they can contact for information about their rights under HIPAA.

4. Tell participants that federal law generally prohibits the plan and health insurance issuers from limiting hospital stays to less than 48 hours for natural deliveries and 96 hours for cesarean sections.

The disclosure changes must be in place within 60 days after the beginning of the next plan year after July 1, 1997. If the plan operates on a calendar basis, there is a 60-day window after January 1, 1998 to make new disclosures to staff members.[3]

The federal government has posted revised guidance and a pamphlet for implementing HIPAA on the Web at www.dol.gov/dol//topic/health-plans/portability.htm. A pamphlet can be obtained by calling the Pension and Welfare Benefits Administration Publication Hotline (1-800-998-7542). See the box for questions and answers regarding new regulations for the Newborns' and Mothers' Health Protection Act, the Mental Health Parity Act, and the Women's Health and Cancer Rights Act of 1998.

THE NEWBORNS' AND MOTHERS' HEALTH PROTECTION ACT OF 1996

Questions and Answers

The Newborns' and Mothers' Health Protection Act of 1996 (the Newborns' Act) was signed into law on September 26, 1996. The law includes important new protections for mothers and their newborn children with regard to the length of hospital stay following childbirth. The Newborns' Act is subject to concurrent jurisdiction by the Departments of Labor, the Treasury, and Health and Human Services.

On October 27, 1998 the Departments of Labor, the Treasury, and Health and Human Services issued interim regulations that interpret the provisions of the Newborns' Act. These regulations clarify the statutory requirements and provide information valuable to employers and employees in understanding their rights and obligations under the law.

The following information is intended to provide general guidance on frequently asked questions about the Newborns' Act.

(continues)

I am a pregnant woman. How does the Newborns' Act affect my health care benefits?

The Newborns' Act affects the amount of time you and your newborn child are covered for a hospital stay following childbirth. Group health plans, insurance companies, and health maintenance organizations (HMOs) that are subject to the Newborns' Act may not restrict benefits for a hospital stay in connection with childbirth to less than 48 hours following a vaginal delivery or 96 hours following a delivery by cesarean section. However, the attending provider may decide, after consulting with you, to discharge you or your newborn child earlier. In any case, the attending provider cannot receive incentives to discharge you or your child earlier than 48 hours (or 96 hours).

Who is the attending provider?

An attending provider is an individual licensed under state law who is directly responsible for providing maternity or pediatric care to a mother or newborn child. Therefore, a plan, hospital, insurance company, or HMO would not be an attending provider. However, a nurse, midwife, or a physician assistant may be an attending provider if licensed in the state to provide maternity or pediatric care in connection with childbirth.

Under the Newborns' Act, when does the 48-hour (or 96-hour) period start?

If you deliver in the hospital, the 48-hour period (or 96-hour period) starts at the time of delivery.

Example: A pregnant woman covered under a group health plan goes into labor and is admitted to the hospital at 10 P.M. on June 11. She gives birth by vaginal delivery at 6 A.M. on June 12. In this example, the 48-hour period begins at 6 A.M. on June 12.

However, if you deliver outside the hospital and you are later admitted to the hospital in connection with childbirth (as determined by the attending provider), the period begins at the time of the admission.

Example: A woman covered under a group health plan gives birth at home by vaginal delivery. After the delivery, the woman begins bleeding excessively in connection with childbirth and is admitted to the hospital. In this example, the 48-hour period starts at the time of admission.

Under the Newborns' Act, may a group health plan, insurance company, or HMO require me to get permission (sometimes called prior authorization or precertification based upon medical necessity) for a 48- or 96-hour hospital stay?

A plan, insurance company, or HMO cannot deny you or your newborn child coverage for a 48-hour stay (or 96-hour stay) because the plan claims that you have failed to show that the 48-hour stay (or 96-hour stay) is medically necessary.

Example: In the case of a delivery by cesarean section, a plan requires patients to call a utilization reviewer to obtain precertification for a hospital length of stay based on a determination of medical necessity. In this example, if the plan's utilization reviewer denies a mother or her newborn benefits within the 96-hour stay, the plan would have violated the Newborns' Act.

Also, plans, insurance companies, and HMOs may not require your attending provider to complete a certificate of medical necessity in order to cover any part of a 48-hour (or 96- hour) stay.

Example: In the case of a delivery by cesarean section, a plan automatically pays for the first 72 hours. For a longer stay, the plan requires the attending provider to complete a certificate of medical necessity, which the plan uses to determine whether a longer stay is medically necessary. In this example, the requirement that a provider complete a certificate of medical necessity to obtain authorization for the period between 72 hours and 96 hours following delivery is prohibited.

However, plans, insurance companies, and HMOs generally can require you to notify the plan of the pregnancy in advance of an admission if you wish to use certain providers or facilities, or to reduce your out-of-pocket costs.

Example: A group health plan generally covers 70 percent of the cost of a hospital stay in connection with childbirth. However, the plan will cover 80 percent of the cost of the stay if you call and notify the plan of your pregnancy in advance of admission and use whatever participating hospital the plan designates. In this example, the plan's notification requirement is permissible. (For more information on cost sharing, see the next question and answer.)

(continues)

Under the Newborns' Act, may group health plans, insurance companies, or HMOs impose deductibles or other cost-sharing provisions for hospital stays in connection with childbirth?

Yes, but only if the deductible, coinsurance, or other cost-sharing provision for the latter part of a 48-hour (or 96-hour) stay are not greater than that imposed for the earlier part of the stay. For example, with respect to a 48-hour stay, a group health plan is permitted to cover only 80 percent of the cost of the hospital stay. However, a plan covering 80 percent of the cost of the first 24 hours could not reduce coverage to 50 percent for the second 24 hours.

Does the Newborns' Act apply to my coverage?

It depends. The Newborns' Act does not apply to all coverage. First, the Newborns' Act applies only to plans, insurance companies, and HMOs that offer benefits in connection with childbirth. In other words, the Newborns' Act does not require plans to offer such coverage.

Second, if your plan offers these benefits, the Newborns' Act only applies to certain coverage. Specifically, it depends on whether your coverage is "insured" by an insurance company or HMO or "self-insured" by the employment-based plan. (You should check your Summary Plan Description [SPD] or contact your plan administrator to find out if your coverage in connection with childbirth is insured or self-insured.)

Self-insured coverage is subject to the Newborns' Act. However, if your coverage is insured by an insurance company or HMO, and your state has a law regulating coverage for newborns and mothers that meets specific criteria, then your rights depend on state law, rather than the Newborns' Act. If this is the case, the state law may differ slightly from the Newborns' Act requirements, so it is important for you to know which law applies to your coverage in order to know what your rights are.

Based on a preliminary review of state laws as of July 1, 1998, the following states and other jurisdictions have a law regulating coverage for newborns and mothers that would apply to coverage insured by an insurance company or HMO:

Alabama, Alaska, Arizona, Arkansas, California, Colorado, Connecticut, the District of Columbia, Florida, Georgia, Illinois, Indiana, Iowa, Kansas, Kentucky, Louisiana, Maine, Maryland, Massachusetts, Minnesota, Missouri, Montana, Nevada, New Hampshire, New Jersey, New Mexico, New York, North Carolina, North Dakota, Ohio, Oklahoma, Pennsylvania, Rhode Island, South Carolina, South Dakota, Tennessee, Texas, Virginia, Washington and West Virginia.

If your coverage is insured by an insurance company or HMO, you should always contact your State Insurance Commissioner's Office for the most current information on state laws.

If the Newborns' Act applies to my coverage, when do its requirements go into effect?

The Newborns' Act's requirements apply to group health plans for plan years beginning on or after January 1, 1998. To find out when your plan year begins, check your Summary Plan Description (SPD) or contact your plan administrator.[4]

THE MENTAL HEALTH PARITY ACT OF 1996

Questions and Answers

The Mental Health Parity Act (MHPA) was signed into law on September 26, 1996. MHPA provides for parity in the application of aggregate lifetime and annual dollar limits on mental health benefits with dollar limits on medical/surgical benefits, MHPA's provisions are subject to concurrent jurisdiction by the Departments of Labor, the Treasury, and Health and Human Services.

On December 22, 1997, the Departments of Labor, the Treasury, and Health and Human Services issued interim regulations that interpret MHPA. The regulations clarify the statutory requirements and provide information valuable to employers and employees in understanding their obligations and rights under the law.

The following information is intended to provide general guidance on frequently asked questions about MHPA.

How will the Mental Health Parity Act affect my benefits?

Under MHPA, group health plans, insurance companies, and HMOs offering mental health benefits will no longer be allowed to set annual or lifetime dollar limits on mental health benefits that are lower than any such dollar limits for medical and surgical benefits. A plan that does not impose an annual or lifetime dollar limit on medical and surgical benefits may not impose such a dollar limit on mental health benefits offered under the plan. MHPA's provisions, however, do not apply to benefits for substance abuse or chemical dependency.

(continues)

Will MHPA require all health plans to provide mental health benefits?

No. Health plans are not required to include mental health in their benefits package. The requirements under MHPA apply only to plans offering mental health benefits.

May a plan impose other restrictions on mental health benefits?

Yes. Plans will still be able to set the terms and conditions (such as cost sharing and limits on the number of visits or days of coverage) for the amount, duration, and scope of mental health benefits.

Do all plans offering mental health benefits have to meet the parity requirements?

No. There are two exceptions to these new rules. First, the mental health parity requirements do not apply to small employers who have fewer than 51 employees. Second, any group health plan whose costs increase 1 percent or more due to the application of MHPA's requirements may claim an exemption from MHPA's requirements.

How does a plan claim the 1 percent increased cost exemption under MHPA?

The increased cost exemption must be taken based on actual claims data, not on an increase in insurance premiums. The provisions of MHPA must be implemented for at least six months and the calculation of the 1 percent cost exemption must be based on at least six months of actual claims data with parity in place. In addition:

- Plans claiming the increased cost exemption must notify the appropriate government agency and plan participants and beneficiaries 30 days before the exemption becomes effective.

- A formula is provided for plans to calculate the increased cost of complying with parity.

- A summary of the aggregate data and the computation supporting the increased cost exemption must be made available to plan participants and beneficiaries free of charge upon written request.

- Once a plan qualifies for the 1 percent increased cost exemption, it does not have to comply with the parity requirements for the life of the MHPA provisions, which sunset on September 30, 2001.

When do the mental health parity requirements take effect? Are these changes permanent?

The mental health parity requirements apply to group health plans for plan years beginning on or after January 1, 1998. Plans that have calendar year plan years or plan years that otherwise begin early in 1998 were provided a transition period until March 31, 1998, when the federal government will not take enforcement action against plans that have sought to comply in good faith with the requirements of the law and need the extra time to modify their plans to conform with the requirements under MHPA.

Plans that chose to utilize the transition period to come into full compliance were required to notify the federal government within 30 days of the beginning of their plan year (but no later than March 31, 1998) regarding their intent to use the transition period to achieve compliance.

Under MHPA, there is also a "sunset" provision requiring that the law will cease to apply to benefits for services furnished on or after September 30, 2001.[5]

THE WOMEN'S HEALTH AND CANCER RIGHTS ACT OF 1998

Questions and Answers

The Women's Health and Cancer Rights Act (Women's Health Act) was signed into law on October 21, 1998. The law includes important new protections for breast cancer patients who elect breast reconstruction in connection with a mastectomy. The Women's Health Act amended the Employee Retirement Income Security Act of 1974 (ERISA) and the Public Health Service (PHS) Act and is administered by the Departments of Labor and Health and Human Services.

The following information is intended to provide general guidance on frequently asked questions about the Women's Health Act provisions that amend ERISA.

I've been diagnosed with breast cancer and plan to have a mastectomy. How will the Women's Health Act affect my benefits?

Under the Women's Health Act, group health plans, insurance companies, and health maintenance organizations (HMOs) offering mastectomy

(continues)

coverage must also provide coverage for reconstructive surgery in a manner determined in consultation with the attending physician and the patient. Coverage includes reconstruction of the breast on which the mastectomy was performed, surgery, and reconstruction of the other breast to produce a symmetrical appearance, and prostheses and treatment of physical complications at all stages of the mastectomy, including lymphedemas.

Will the Women's Health Act require all group health plans, insurance companies, and HMOs to provide reconstructive surgery benefits?

All group health plans and their insurance companies or HMOs that provide coverage for medical and surgical benefits with respect to a mastectomy are subject to the requirements of the Women's Health Act.

Under the Women's Health Act, may group health plans, insurance companies, or HMOs impose deductibles or coinsurance requirements for reconstructive surgery in connection with a mastectomy?

Yes, but only if the deductibles and coinsurance are consistent with those established for other benefits under the plan or coverage.

When do these requirements take effect?

The reconstructive surgery requirements apply to group health plans for plan years beginning on or after October 21, 1998. To find out when your plan year begins, check your Summary Plan Description (SPD) or contact your plan administrator.

These requirements also apply to individual health insurance policies offered, sold, issued, renewed, in effect, or operated on or after October 21, 1998. These requirements were placed in the PHS Act within the jurisdiction of the Department of Health and Human Services.

My state requires the coverage for breast reconstruction that is required by the Women's Health Act and also requires minimum hospital stays in connection with a mastectomy that are not required by the Women's Health Act. If I have a mastectomy and breast reconstruction, am I also entitled to the minimum hospital stay?

It depends. The federal Women's Health Act permits state law protections to apply to certain health coverage. State law protections apply if the state law is in effect on October 21, 1998 (date of enactment of the Women's Health Act) and the state law requires at least the coverage for reconstructive breast surgery that is required by the federal Women's Health Act.

If state law meets these requirements, then it applies to coverage provided by an insurance company or HMO ("insured" coverage). If you obtained your coverage through your employer and your coverage is insured, you would be entitled to the minimum hospital stay required by state law. If you obtained your coverage through your employer but your coverage is not provided by an insurance company or HMO (that is, your employer "self-insures" your coverage), then state law does not apply. In that case, only the federal Women's Health Act applies and it does not require minimum hospital stays. To find out if your group health coverage is insured or self-insured, check your Summary Plan Description (SPD) or contact your plan administrator.

If you obtained your coverage under a private individual health insurance policy (not through your employer), check with your State Insurance Commissioner's office to learn if state law applies.

The Women's Health Act also requires that group health plans, insurance companies, and HMOs provide two notices regarding the coverage required by the Women's Health Act.

Are all group health plans, and their insurance companies and HMOs, required to satisfy the notice requirements under the Women's Health Act?

All group health plans and their insurance companies or HMOs that offer coverage for medical and surgical benefits with respect to a mastectomy are subject to the notice requirements under the Women's Health Act.

What are the notice requirements under the Women's Health Act?

There are two separate notices required under the Women's Health Act. The first notice is a one-time requirement under which group health plans and their insurance companies or HMOs must furnish a written description of the benefits that the Women's Health Act requires. The second notice must also describe the benefits required under the Women's Health Act, but it must be provided upon enrollment in the plan, and it must be furnished annually thereafter.

How must these notices be delivered to participants and beneficiaries?

These notices must be delivered in accordance with the Department of Labor's disclosure regulations applicable to furnishing summary plan descriptions. (29 CFR § 2520.104b-1).

(continues)

For example, the notices may be provided by first-class mail or any other means of delivery prescribed in the regulation. It is the view of the department that a separate notice would be required to be furnished to a group health plan beneficiary when the last known address of the beneficiary is different than the last known address of the covered participant.

When must the initial one-time notice under the Women's Health Act be furnished to participants and beneficiaries?

The one-time notice must be furnished as part of the next general mailing (made after October 21, 1998) by the group health plan and their insurance companies or HMOs or in the yearly informational packet sent out regarding the plan, but in no event can the one-time notice be furnished later than January 1, 1999.

Does a group health plan that already provided the coverage required by the Women's Health Act have to send out the initial one-time notice?

A group health plan that, prior to the date of enactment (October 21, 1998), already provided the coverage required by the Women's Health Act (and continues to provide such coverage) will have satisfied the initial one-time notice requirement if the information required to be provided in the initial notice was previously furnished to participants and beneficiaries in accordance with the department's regulations on disclosure of information to participants and beneficiaries.

What information must be included in the Women's Health Act notices?

The notices must describe the benefits that the Women's Health Act requires the group health plan and its insurance companies or HMOs to cover. The notice must indicate that, in the case of a participant or beneficiary who is receiving benefits under the plan in connection with a mastectomy and who elects breast reconstruction, the coverage will be provided in a manner determined in consultation with the attending physician and the patient, for:

- reconstruction of the breast on which the mastectomy was performed;
- surgery and reconstruction of the other breast to produce a symmetrical appearance;
- and prostheses and treatment of physical complications at all stages of the mastectomy, including lymphedemas.

The notice must also describe any deductibles and coinsurance limitations applicable to such coverage. Under the Women's Health Act, coverage of breast reconstruction benefits may be subject only to deductibles and coinsurance limitations consistent with those established for other benefits under the plan or coverage.

Must a group health plan and their insurance companies or HMOs furnish separate notices under the Women's Health Act?

No. To avoid duplication of notices, a group health plan or its insurance companies or HMOs can satisfy the notice requirements of the Women's Health Act by contracting with another party that provides the required notice. For example, in the case of a group health plan funded through an insurance policy, the group health plan will satisfy the notice requirements with respect to a participant or beneficiary if the insurance company or HMO actually provides the notice that includes the information required by the Women's Health Act.[6]

Policy

EXHIBIT 4.6   **CERTIFICATE OF GROUP HEALTH PLAN COVERAGE**

Important: This certificate provides evidence of your prior health coverage. You may need to furnish this certificate if you become eligible under a group health plan that excludes coverage for certain medical conditions that you have before you enroll. This certificate may need to be provided if medical advice, diagnosis, care, or treatment was recommended or received for the condition within the six-month period prior to your enrollment in the new plan. If you become covered under another group health plan, check with the plan administrator to see if you need to provide this certificate. You also may need this certificate to buy an insurance policy for yourself or your family that does not exclude coverage for medical conditions that are present before you enroll.

1. Date of this certificate:

   _____

2. Name of group health plan:

   _____

3. Name of participant:

   _____

(continues)

EXHIBIT 4.6   CONTINUED

4. Identification number of participant:

_____

5. Name of any dependents to whom this certificate applies:

_____

6. Name, address, and telephone number of plan administrator or issuer responsible for providing this certificate:

_____

_____

_____

7. For further information call:

_____

8. If the individual(s) identified in line 3 and line 5 has at least 18 months of creditable coverage (disregarding periods of coverage before a 63-day break), check here _____ and skip lines 9 and 10.

9. Date waiting period or affiliation period (if any) began:

_____

10. Date coverage began: _____

11. Date coverage ended: _____ (or check if coverage is continuing as of the date of this certificate: _____)

Note: Separate certificates will be furnished if information is not identical for the participant and each beneficiary.[7]

WORKERS' COMPENSATION

Rationale

All states have some version of a workers' compensation law. The laws require employees to carry insurance against loss of income due to injury or death that occurs during work activities. Check with the state in which a nonprofit is incorporated and, if different, the state where offices are located to learn what workers' compensation laws are applicable. In Colorado, such laws are administered by the Department of Labor.

The laws set up a system, outside of civil lawsuits, to give workers security that they will get benefits if they are injured on the job. Fault does not need to be established. Employees give up the right to sue the employer for negligence when covered under this law. The employer pays for workers' compensation insurance, and the insurance carrier pays the benefits. Employers are required to post notices about the law and the coverage where employees will see them. Staff members must report all job-related accidents, injuries, and illness in writing within four days after which they occur. Depending on the seriousness of the situation, employers must report time missed from work to the appropriate government agency.

Anyone the nonprofit pays for work is covered except when the employee is actually working for another organization, such as a temporary labor agency. Volunteers usually are not covered, but they might be under certain conditions. Also, a person in job training placements might be. State law must be checked to determine who is covered specifically.[8]

EMPLOYEE ASSISTANCE PROGRAM

Rationale

Employees may have personal problems that affect job performance. The problems may be substance abuse, situational, or due to emotional disorders or mental illness. Many employers have Employee Assistance Programs (EAPs) that are a resource troubled employees can access for help to resolve their problems. It is also a help to the employer to have professional and confidential assistance to which to refer the employee. The supervisor's job is to identify job performance issues, determine that they may be related to personal problems, and offer a referral to the EAP. An employee cannot be forced to use the EAP resource. The supervisor should document the attempt to refer and the employee's decision to accept help or not. At the same time, the supervisor must ensure that the employee understands and agrees to address job performance concerns and meet expectations so the nonprofit organization obtains the benefits needed from the employee's contribution to the mission of the organization.

Policy

This nonprofit recognizes that a variety of personal problems or situations may interfere with the ability of an individual staff member to perform satisfactorily while on the job. In responding constructively to these problems, it is this nonprofit's intention to restore the job effectiveness of the staff member and to make it possible for the individual to get the help they need.

Procedures

- This nonprofit supports referral and rehabilitation efforts extended to staff members affected by personal problems or situations. No staff member's job security or promotional opportunity will be put in jeopardy by their seeking and conscientiously following a program of treatment.

- Supervisory personnel are expected to recognize difficulties based strictly on unsatisfactory job performance resulting from apparent behavior or personal problems.

- This nonprofit will make available the name, address, and phone number of outside agencies that offer or make referrals for treatment. Staff members who suspect they have a problem are urged to take advantage of the Employee Assistance Program and voluntarily follow through with any prescribed treatment.

- When the behavior of a staff member undergoing treatment results in poor job performance, it will be handled in the same manner as any other substandard performance.

- Reporting to work under the influence of drugs or alcohol, or possession of drugs or alcohol on the nonprofit's property, will result in immediate dismissal.

- Voluntary acceptance of a treatment program does not negate requirements regarding job performance.

SPENDING ACCOUNTS

Rationale

Pretax spending accounts are a low-cost benefit that can be offered to employees. Employees can elect to have pretax earnings placed into such an account for health care, dependent day care, and uninsured care costs. The plans do require help from a professional to set up, and small administrative costs may be involved. The nonprofit organization should be sure the spending accounts policy explains how and when deductions are made, what types of expenditures employees can draw against the spending account to pay, any dollar limits on the amounts that can be set aside, and what happens to the money placed in the account if it is not used by the end of the year.

An account or benefits consultant can provide more information on how to set up a spending account program.

DENTAL INSURANCE

Rationale

Health insurance as a benefit offered by employers is perhaps more important today than ever with individually purchased coverage so hard to obtain and afford. Dental insurance may be included as health plan benefit or through a separate dental policy. It is a good idea to survey staff members to see how much value they place on a dental insurance plan. Employers may wish to control rapidly rising health insurance costs so there may be trade-offs to consider in terms of the total package of health-related benefits.

LIFE AND DISABILITY

Disability Plans

Rationale

A disability insurance benefit pays employees some portion of their salary if they must miss long periods of work due to illness or injury. The benefits are defined in the plan including such features as how soon the insurance will be available, what proof of disability is required, what the benefit is, and how long payments will be made. There is a difference between short- and long-term disabilities. Short-term absences due to illness or injury often are covered by use of accumulated sick leave, annual leave, and personal leave days. Disability insurance not only benefits employees at the time they need it the most, but it also provides a way for employers to support an employee during sickness or injury that does not expose the employer to moral dilemmas or budget concerns.

Life Insurance

Rationale

An employer-offered life insurance policy that will provide a death benefit is common and considered by some to be a basic in employee benefit packages. The employer commonly pays the premium in full, or the employee may participate by contributing to the premium. Portability of the policy is an important feature to consider. Being able to continue the policy when they leave employment makes the benefit more useful to employees. It may be especially important to older employees who may have more trouble obtaining life insurance policies on their own at affordable rates.

401(k), 403(b), and Section 457 Plans

Rationale

According to Joan E. Pynes, author, *Human Resources Management for Public and Nonprofit Organizations*, deferred compensation plans offer employees employer-assisted savings plans.

> The 401(k) plan is a deferred compensation plan in which employees can elect to have the employer contribute a portion of wages to the plan on a pre-tax basis. These deferred wages are not subject to income tax withholding at the time of deferral. They are included as wages subject to social security, Medicare, and federal unemployment taxes. The amount that can be contributed is limited, for 2003 the limit was $12,000 for all 401(k) plans in which the employee participates. If the employee participates in a SIMPLE 401K plan, the limit in 2003 was $8000. Limits are indexed for inflation and can be expected to change. Some employers match the employee contribution at a limited rate.
>
> IRC 501c3 designated nonprofits may also provide employees to defer some of their salary into the Section 403 (b) tax-sheltered plan sponsored by their employer. IRC 457 plans are available for non-governmental entities tax exempt under IRC 501. They can be either eligible plans under IRC 457(b) or ineligible plans under IRC 457(f). Plans eligible under 457(b) allow employees of sponsoring organizations to defer income taxation on retirement savings into future years. Ineligible plans may trigger different tax treatment under 457(f).[9]

It is best to contact a specialist when considering setting up these plans as their administration is regulated, and it is necessary to follow the regulations very carefully to avoid violations and penalties. The IRS Web site, www.irs.gov/retirement, explains the plans and provides information on how they must be administered.

LEAVE

Vacation

Rationale

Vacation leave usually is earned on a monthly basis and allowed to accrue for a year. Some leave may be carried over between years. Calendar years or fiscal years often define the accrual period rather than the employee's hire date. Employers should be aware that they must pay accrued leave when an employment terminates for any cause, and thus accrued leave is a financial liability. Limiting this liability is one reason why employers limit the amount of accrual and require leave to be taken in the year in which it was earned. Another reason is that it is healthy for employees to take vacation days, and healthy employees are often more productive and contribute to a positive workplace environment. Part-time staff accrue vacation days on a prorated basis.

The amount of leave earned per month may be greater as length of employment grows. As an example, a new staff person may earn 1 day of leave per month for a total of 12 days per year. This may increase to 15 days per month after the fifth year. Another increase in rate of earned leave may occur at other longevity milestones. There also may be differences in rate of leave earned between exempt and nonexempt employees. Because nonexempt employees must be paid overtime and exempt employees generally are not paid overtime, exempt employees may have a richer leave benefit to compensate them indirectly for the extra hours worked without additional pay. Policies on compensatory time off for exempt employees working overtime may influence if and how much the nonprofit wants to enrich their leave benefit.

Vacation requests should be made in advance in writing. Requests are granted upon approval of the supervisor and are subject to the needs of the organization.

Some surveys of nonprofit compensation include leave benefits and may provide valuable comparison information.

Holidays

Rationale

Traditional holidays include:

New Year's Day

President's Day

Martin Luther King, Jr. Day

Good Friday

Memorial Day

Fourth of July

Labor Day

Thanksgiving

Christmas

To accommodate personal religious and ethnic diversity, it is common to add a couple of personal leave days to the list of official holidays. The holiday policy should explain what happens when the holiday falls on a weekend. Usually, if the holiday falls on a Saturday, the Friday before the holiday is a non-work day. Likewise, if the holiday falls on a Sunday, the following Monday is a non-work day. Commonly, staff cannot accrue unused holidays, and holidays cannot be converted into cash benefits.

Holidays and Overtime Pay and/or Compensatory Time

Rationale

Due to their missions, many organizations may need to have staff coverage on legal holidays. Some kind of compensation incentive may be offered for employees who work on holidays. Because which employees work holidays will vary, the compensation should not affect the base salary for the job the employee is hired to perform. Rather, the additional compensation should be administered as an add-on to the base salary for authorized pay for holidays worked. Compensatory time off can be the compensation of choice for exempt employees. Nonexempt employees would have to take the compensatory day off within the same one-week period if the employer does not wish to pay overtime pay.

Floating Personal Days

Rationale

Many nonprofits offer one or two personal floating holidays a year. These are days off that an employee can use for any reason. Personal days are subject to the needs of the nonprofit organization and must be approved in advance by the employee's supervisor. Part-time employees receive a prorated leave benefit based on the percentage of full time they work. This benefit is often subject to a waiting period of three to six months after employment. The organization may wish to limit the benefit for an employee hired later in the year. For example, a person hired halfway through the calendar year would have one personal day to use rather than two. Staff members are not paid for unused personal days if they leave the organization, as they are not accrued and cannot be converted into cash payments.

Sick Leave

Rationale

Sick leave is earned on a pay period basis, often at one day a month. Nonprofits may wish to enrich the amount of sick leave earned. The policy should state when and how sick leave accrues, as well as the conditions under which it may or may not be used. Acceptable use of sick leave has broadened to include preventive health care, mental health days, and care for a sick or injured family member. The policy should state the organization's right to ask for a doctor's excuse for extended illnesses or a pattern of illness. A ceiling for accrual of sick leave may be part of the policy. The organization should state whether sick leave can be converted to cash or other leave. This decision may affect the financial liability of the nonprofit. Advice from an accountant on this matter is recommended before a policy is adopted regarding conversion. Part-time employees earn sick leave on a prorated basis. Employees should be required to notify their supervisor at the start of a sick period or in advance if the purpose of sick leave is known prior to use.

BENEFIT PLANS

FAMILY AND MEDICAL LEAVE

Rationale

The Family and Medical Leave Act (FMLA) effects all nonprofits with 50 or more employees at a single site or at one or more sites within a 75-mile radius. The FMLA lists eligibility, and defines child, parent, spouse, and serious health condition as well. The policy clearly states the procedure staff must follow to request leaves for each of the eligibility categories. The policy also gives the status of benefits during leave, job reassignment, the procedure staff members must follow when returning to work, and the penalties for not returning to work, or failing to contact the employer at the scheduled time.

To help with the administrative aspect of family leave, the policy requires all staff members requesting leave to complete a Request for FMLA Leave of Absence form. The employer might provide employees with a brochure to achieve understanding of rights and responsibilities under the FMLA (see Exhibits 4.7 and 4.8).

Policy

The purpose of this policy is to provide leaves of absence to eligible staff members in accordance with the Family and Medical Leave Act of 1993.

This policy applies to all staff members who have worked at the nonprofit for at least one year at the time the leave is requested and have completed at least 1,250 hours of service during the 12-month period preceding the leave request, and work at a site where at least 50 staff members are employed, or within a 75-mile radius of that site. Eligible staff may be granted up to 12 weeks' unpaid leave in any 12-month period.

For the birth of a staff member's child, or upon placement of a child with the staff member for adoption or foster care, a leave of absence is provided. This leave will normally be taken in one block of time unless the employer approves special arrangements for "intermittent" or "reduced work schedule."

When the staff member is needed to care for a child, spouse, or parent who has a serious health condition.

When the staff member is unable to perform their functions due to a serious health condition.

Applicable accrued leave benefits must be substituted for all or part of any otherwise unpaid FMLA leave. The total of paid and unpaid leave under this policy is not to exceed 12 weeks.

For the purposes of this policy, the following definitions will serve:

Child: Anyone under 18 years who is the staff member's biological, adopted or foster child, stepchild, legal ward, or an adult legally dependent child. This may include a child for whom the employee has day-to-day responsibility.

Parent: Biological, foster or adoptive parents, stepparents, legal guardians, or any individual who stood in place of parents for a staff member when the staff member was a child.

Spouse: A husband or wife as defined by applicable state law.

Serious health condition: An illness, injury, impairment, or physical or mental condition that involves inpatient care, or any period of incapacity requiring absence from school or work of more than three calendar days, and involving continuing treatment by a health care provider.

Requesting Family or Medical Leave Procedure

A Request for FMLA Leave of Absence form must be completed by a staff member requesting leave, and submitted 30 days before commencement date. If 30 days' advance notice is not possible, FMLA leave must be given as soon as possible.

When the leave is due to a staff member or family member's serious health condition, the staff member must provide a Certification of Serious Health Condition form [see Exhibit 4.7] completed by the health care provider.

Recertification of the serious health condition may be required during leave.

While on leave, staff members are required to contact the employer every 15 days to advise of any change or improvement in condition.

When the leave is for planned medical treatment, the staff member must attempt to schedule the treatment so as not to disrupt the nonprofit's operations.

Status of Benefits during Leave

During leave under this policy, the staff member is responsible for any insurance payments normally deducted through payroll. These payment obligations must be explained to the staff person prior to beginning leave or when the leave is not planned in advance, when the FMLA is approved.

If a staff member fails to return to work at the end of the leave, the nonprofit may recover from the staff member the cost of any payments made to maintain the staff member's coverage, unless the failure to return was beyond their control.

A staff member on leave will not lose any employment benefits accrued prior to leave, unless the staff member uses a benefit during the leave, such as accrued annual or sick leave. Sick and annual leave and seniority does not accrue while a staff member is on family and medical leave.

Return to Work

Before being permitted to return to work from a leave for the staff member's own serious health condition, the staff member will be required to provide certification from their health care provider that they are able to resume work.

Upon return from leave, most staff members will be reinstated in the following priority of position reassignment: if available, the same position held before leave, or reassignment to an equivalent position with equivalent pay, benefits, and other conditions of employment.

If possible, staff members on leave should notify their supervisor at least two weeks before the end of the leave to inform the nonprofit of availability to return to work.

Failure to return from leave, or failure to contact a supervisor on the scheduled date of return, may be considered voluntary termination of employment.[10]

FMLA Compliance

(a) FMLA provides that covered employers shall make, keep, and preserve records pertaining to their obligations under the Act in accordance with the record keeping requirements of section 11(c) of the Fair Labor Standards Act (FLSA) and in accordance with these regulations, FMLA also restricts the authority of the Department of Labor to require any employer or plan, fund, or program to submit books or records more than once during any 12-month period unless the DOL has reasonable cause to believe a violation of the FMLA exists or the DOL is investigating a complaint. These regulations establish no requirement for the submission of any records unless specifically requested by a departmental official.

(b) Form of records. No particular order or form of records is required. These regulations establish no requirement that any employer revise its computerized payroll or personnel records systems to comply. However, employers must keep the records specified by these regulations for no less than three years and make them available for inspection, copying, and transcription by representatives of the Department of Labor upon request. The records may be maintained and preserved on microfilm or other basic source document of an automated data processing memory provided that adequate projection or viewing equipment is available, that the reproductions are clear and identifiable by date or pay period, and that extensions or transcriptions of the information required herein can be and are made available upon request. Records kept in computer form must be made available for transcription or copying.

(c) Items required. Covered employers who have eligible employees must maintain records that must disclose the following:

(1) Basic payroll and identifying employee data, including name, address, and occupation; rate or basis of pay and terms of compensation; daily and weekly hours worked per pay period; additions to or deductions from wages; and total compensation paid.

(2) Dates FMLA leave is taken by FMLA eligible employees (e.g., available from time records, requests for leave, etc., if so designated).

Leave must be designated in records as FMLA leave; leave so designated may not include leave required under state law or an employer plan which is not also covered by FMLA.

(3) If FMLA leave is taken by eligible employees in increments of less than one full day, the hours of the leave.

(4) Copies of employee notices of leave furnished to the employer under FMLA, if in writing, and copies of all general and specific written notices given to employees as required under FMLA and these regulations (see Sec. 825.301(b)). Copies may be maintained in employee personnel files.

(5) Any documents (including written and electronic records) describing employee benefits or employer policies and practices regarding the taking of paid and unpaid leaves.

(6) Premium payments of employee benefits.

(7) Records of any dispute between the employer and an eligible employee regarding designation of leave as FMLA leave, including any written statement from the employer or employee of the reasons for the designation and for the disagreement.

(d) Covered employers with no eligible employees must maintain the records set forth in paragraph (c) (1) above.

(e) Covered employers in a joint employment situation (see Sec. 825.106) must keep all the records required by paragraph (c) of this section with respect to any primary employees, and must keep the records required by paragraph (c) (1) with respect to any secondary employees.

(f) If FMLA-eligible employees are not subject to FLSA's record keeping regulations for purposes of minimum wage or overtime compliance (i.e., not covered by or exempt from FLSA), an employer need not keep a record of actual hours worked (as otherwise required under FLSA, 29 CFR 516.2(a) (7)), provided that:

(1) Eligibility for FMLA leave is presumed for any employee who has been employed for at least 12 months; and

(2) With respect to employees who take FMLA leave intermittently or on a reduced leave schedule, the employer and employee agree on the employee's normal schedule or average hours worked each week and reduce their agreement to a written record maintained in accordance with paragraph (b) of this section.

(g) Records and documents relating to medical certifications, re-certifications, or medical histories of employees or employees' family members, created for purposes of FMLA, shall be maintained as confidential medical records in separate files/records from the usual personnel files, and if ADA is also applicable, such records shall be maintained in conformance with ADA confidentiality requirements (see 29 CFR Sec. 1630.14(c) (1)), except that:

(1) Supervisors and managers may be informed regarding necessary restrictions on the work or duties of an employee and necessary accommodations;

(2) First aid and safety personnel may be informed (when appropriate) if the employee's physical or medical condition might require emergency treatment; and

(3) Government officials investigating compliance with FMLA (or other pertinent law) shall be provided relevant information upon request.[11]

EXHIBIT 4.7   CERTIFICATION OF HEALTH CARE PROVIDER

Certification of Health Care Provider (Family and Medical Leave Act of 1993)	U.S. Department of Labor Employment Standards Administration Wage and Hour Division
	OMB No.: 1215-0181 Expires: 06-30-02
1. Employee's Name	2. Patient's Name (if different from employee)

3. The attached sheet describes what is meant by a "serious health condition" under the Family and Medical Act. Does the patient's condition qualify under any of the categories described?[1] If so, please check

(1) ___ (2) ___ (3) ___ (4) ___ (5) ___ (6) ___, or None of the above ___

4. Describe the medical facts which support your certification, including a brief statement as to how the medical facts meet the criteria of one of these categories:

EXHIBIT 4.7   CONTINUED

5. a. State the approximate date the condition commenced, and the probable duration of the condition (and also the probable duration of the patient's present incapacity,[2] if different):

b. Will it be necessary for the employee to take work only intermittently or to work on a less than full schedule as a result of the condition (including for treatment described in Item 6 below)?

If yes, give the probable duration:

c. If the condition is a chronic condition (condition #4) or pregnancy, state whether the patient is presently incapacitated and the likely duration and frequency of episodes of incapacity[2]:

---

6. a. If additional treatments will be required for the condition, provide an estimate of the probable number of such treatments:

b. If the patient will be absent from work or other daily activities because of treatment on an intermittent or part-time basis, also provide an estimate of the probable number of and interval between such treatments, actual or estimated dates of treatment if known, and period required for recovery if any:

c. If any of these treatments will be provided by another provider of health services (e.g., physical therapist), please state the nature of the treatments:

Form WH-380

(continues)

EXHIBIT 4.7   CONTINUED

c. **If a regimen of continuing treatment** by the patient is required under your supervision, provide a general description of such regimen (e.g., prescription drugs, physical therapy requiring special equipment):

7. a. If medical leave is required for the employee's **absence from work** because of the **employee's own condition** (including absences due to pregnancy or a chronic condition), is the employee **unable to perform work** of any kind? _____

   b. If able to perform some work, is the employee **unable to perform any one or more of the essential functions of the employee's job** (the employee or the employer should supply you with information about the essential job functions)? _____ If yes, please list the essential functions the employee is unable to perform:

   c. If neither a. nor b. applies, is it necessary for the employee to be **absent from work for treatment?** _____

8. a. If leave is required to **care for a family member** of the employee with a serious health condition, **does the patient require assistance** for basic medical or personal needs or safety, or for transportation? _____
   b. If no, would the employee's presence to provide **psychological comfort** be beneficial to the patient or assist in the patient's recovery? _____
   c. If the patient will need care only intermittently or on a part-time basis, please indicate the probable **duration** of this need:

_____   _____
(Signature of Health Care Provider)   (Type of Practice)

_____   _____
(Address)   (Telephone number)

To be completed by the employee needing family leave to care for a family member.

State the care you will provide and an estimate of the period during which care will be provided, including a schedule if leave is to be taken intermittently or if it will be necessary for you to work less than a full schedule:

_____   _____
(Employee Signature)   (Date)

A "Serious Health Condition" means an illness, injury, impairment, or physical or mental condition that involves one of the following:

1. Hospital Care

Inpatient care (i.e., an overnight stay) in a hospital, hospice, or residential medical care facility, including any period of incapacity[2] or subsequent treatment in connection with or consequent to such inpatient care.

EXHIBIT 4.7   CONTINUED

2. Absence Plus Treatment

(a) A period of incapacity[2] of more than three consecutive calendar days (including any subsequent treatment or period of incapacity[2] relating to the same condition), that also involves:

(1) Treatment[3] two or more times by a health care provider, by a nurse or physician's assistant under direct supervision of a health care provider, or by a provider of health care services (e.g., physical therapist) under orders of, or on referral by, a health care provider; or

(2) Treatment by a health care provider on at least one occasion which results in a regimen of continuing treatment[4] under the supervision of the health care provider.

3. Pregnancy

Any period of incapacity due to pregnancy, or for prenatal care.

4. Chronic Conditions Requiring Treatments

A chronic condition which:

(1) Requires periodic visits for treatment by a health care provider, or by a nurse or physician's assistant under direct supervision of a health care provider;

(2) Continues over an extended period of time (including recurring episodes of a single underlying condition); and

(3) May cause episodic rather than a continuing period of incapacity[2] (e.g., asthma, diabetes, epilepsy, etc.).

5. Permanent/Long-term Conditions Requiring Supervision

A period of incapacity, which is permanent or long-term due to a condition for which treatment may not be effective. The employee or family member must be under the continuing supervision of, but need not be receiving active treatment by, a health care provider. Examples include Alzheimer's, a severe stroke, or the terminal stages of a disease.

6. Multiple Treatments (Non-Chronic Conditions)

Any period of absence to receive multiple treatments (including any period of recovery therefrom) by a health care provider or by a provider of health care services under orders of, or on referral by, a health care provider, either for restorative surgery after an accident or other injury, or for a condition that would likely result in a period of incapacity[2] of more than three consecutive calendar days in the absence of medical intervention or treatment, such as cancer (chemotherapy, radiation, etc.), severe arthritis (physical therapy), and kidney disease (dialysis).

(continues)

EXHIBIT 4.7   CONTINUED

This optional form may be used by employees to satisfy a mandatory requirement to furnish a medical certification (when requested) from a health care provider, including second or third opinions and re-certifications (29 CFR 825.306).

Note: Persons are not required to respond to this collection of information unless it displays a currently valid OMB control number.

---

[1] Here and elsewhere on this form, the information sought relates only to the condition for which the employee is taking FMLA leave.

[2] "Incapacity," for purposes of FMLA, is defined to mean inability to work, attend school, or attend or perform other regular daily activities due to the serious health condition, treatment therefore, or recovery therefrom.

[3] Treatment includes examinations to determine if a serious health condition exists and evaluations of the condition. Treatment does not include routine physical examinations, eye examinations, or dental examinations.

[4] A regimen of continuing treatment includes, for example, a course of prescription medication (e.g., an antibiotic) or therapy requiring special equipment to resolve or alleviate the health condition. A regimen of treatment does not include the taking of over-the-counter medications such as aspirin, antihistamines, or salves; or bed-rest, drinking fluids, exercise, and other similar activities that can be initiated without a visit to a health care provider.

Public Burden Statement

We estimate that it will take an average of 10 minutes to complete this collection of information, including the time for reviewing instructions, searching existing data sources, gathering and maintaining the data needed, and completing and reviewing the collection of information.

Employer Response to Employee   **U.S. Department of Labor**

Request for Family or Medical Leave   Employment Standards Administration

(Optional Use Form—See 29 CFR § 825.301)   Wage and Hour Division

(Family and Medical Leave Act of 1993)

OMB No. : 1215-0181

Date:

Expires: 06-30-02

Source: U.S. Department of Labor, Employment Standards Administration, Wage and Hour Division, Washington, DC, June 1997.

EXHIBIT 4.8   FAMILY/MEDICAL LEAVE REQUEST

To:

_____

(Employee's Name)

From:

_____

(Name of Appropriate Employer Representative)

_____

Subject: **REQUEST FOR FAMILY/MEDICAL LEAVE**

On _____, you notified us of your need to take family/medical leave due to:

(Date)

☐ The birth of a child, or the placement of a child with you for adoption or foster care; or

☐ A serious health condition that makes you unable to perform the essential functions for your job: or

☐ A serious health condition affecting your ☐ spouse, ☐ child, ☐ parent, for which you are needed to provide care.

You notified us that you need this leave beginning on _____ (Date) and that you expect leave to continue until on or about _____. (Date)

Except as explained below, you have a right under the FMLA for up to 12 weeks of unpaid leave in a 12-month period for the reasons listed above. Also, your health benefits must be maintained during any period of unpaid leave under the same conditions as if you continued to work, and you must be reinstated to the same or an equivalent job with the same pay, benefits, and terms and conditions of employment on your return from leave. If you do not return to work following FMLA leave for a reason other than: (1) the continuation, recurrence, or onset of a serious health condition which would entitle you to FMLA leave; or (2) other circumstances beyond your control, you may be required to reimburse us for our share of health insurance premiums paid on your behalf during your FMLA leave.

_____

This is to inform you that: (check appropriate boxes, explain where indicated)

1. You are ☐ eligible ☐ not eligible for leave under the FMLA.

_____

(continues)

EXHIBIT 4.8   CONTINUED

2. The requested leave ☐ will ☐ will not be counted against your annual FMLA leave entitlement.

3. You ☐ will ☐ will not be required to furnish medical certification of a serious health condition. If required, you must furnish certification by _____ (insert date) (must be at least 15 days after you are notified of this requirement), or we may delay the commencement of your leave until the certification is submitted.

4. You may elect to substitute accrued paid leave for unpaid FMLA leave. We ☐ will ☐ will not require that you substitute accrued paid leave for unpaid FMLA leave. If paid leave will be used, the following conditions will apply: (*Explain*)

Source: U.S. Department of Labor, Employment Standards Administration, Wage and Hour Division, Washington, DC, June 1997.

SABBATICAL LEAVE

Rationale

Sabbatical leave in direct service and advocacy nonprofit's is fairly rare, whereas sabbaticals are standard benefits in institutions of higher education. Turnover in executive directors of nonprofits is a severe problem, and burnout is also common. A sabbatical might prevent the loss of a skilled leader, and, depending on how the leave is spent, may provide the executive with new vision and knowledge on how to achieve improved success for the nonprofit. A sabbatical leave policy should state who is eligible, the length of sabbaticals that might be available, other terms for qualification, and any special uses for the sabbatical. The chain of command for approval should be made clear. The sabbatical length can be anything from a summer to a year.

Lack of funding to support the sabbatical leave with pay, the difficulty in redistribution of duties, and lack of general acceptance of sabbaticals as a benefit in direct service and advocacy nonprofits are all barriers to implementing this benefit. Yet it is worth consideration if the nonprofit wishes to motivate and retain talented top managers and professionals, especially executive directors.

Paid Community Service Leave

Rationale

This type of leave fits nonprofit values well. The policy allows employees to perform volunteer community services during paid work time. It can be a motivator to recruit quality staff and for current employees. The policy may be supported by activities sponsored and organized by the nonprofit and/or employees may be able to select the community service in which they are interested. For-profit companies and sometimes government also have community service leave policies (see Exhibit 4.9). An additional reason for adopting such a policy is its contribution to a positive community image and improvement of the larger community through the work of the employee volunteers.

The policy should state the amount of time available for each employee per year and any other restrictions on when the volunteer service can occur. The method for obtaining approval should be clear.

Community service leave should be reported as such on employee time sheets. Nonexempt staff members' time will need to be controlled so community service time does not create an overtime pay situation. Also, community service hours usually are not counted toward granting of compensatory time off for exempt employees.

Policy

EXHIBIT 4.9   REQUEST FOR COMMUNITY SERVICE LEAVE

1. Briefly describe community service and organization you will be volunteering with to perform the service.

2. Please give estimated hours involved in the project and the date(s) and time for each date you expect to be absent from the job.

Staff Member Signature: _____ ,__ Date: _____

For supervisor only

____ Approved ____ Disapproved

Supervisor's Signature: _____ Date: _____

Working Conditions

Pay for Training

Rationale

When a nonprofit requires a staff person to attend training, the time spent in training should be treated as paid work hours. This should be made clear to the staff member. To avoid overtime pay for nonexempt employees, adjustments in the workload and/or reducing work hours by the time spent in training must be done so the total hours worked are 40 or less within a week.

Fees/Honoraria

Rationale

When staff persons make presentations related to the mission of the nonprofit and as a part of its services and a part of their job, the fee or honoraria is paid to the nonprofit organization. This policy is separate from the issue of policies regarding outside employment or other work by employees. If the nonprofit allows employees to engage in paid work outside of work hours, the employee keeps the compensation for that work. If the employee's outside work is closely related to the work of the nonprofit, approval in advance of the work to be performed is a good policy.

Professional Development

Rationale

Investment in the professional growth of staff members is important. Budget allocations for staff training should be made annually. Conferences, seminars, and workshops are all useful. Benefits include improved performance, improved ability to recruit and retain employees, in-house promotion of good employees, and professional networking. Careful attention to selection of professional development programs will align them with the overall goals of the nonprofit and the individual development goals identified through performance reviews and career development plans.

CREDIT UNION MEMBERSHIP

Rationale

Credit union membership made available through the employer as a benefit may help employees access improved loan terms, lower interest rates, and obtain easier, more accessible service. It is a low-cost benefit, and the policy should be simple, explaining the nonprofit's membership in the credit union, who is eligible for membership, and how to enroll in the credit union. Employees should be referred to the credit union for all other information.

BIRTHDAY OFF

Rationale

Nonprofits often are limited in the amount of cash compensation and benefits that they can afford to offer, but they can provide generous leave policies, which is a motivator for many staff persons. Paid leave on employees' birthdays acknowledges them on their special day. Birthday leave might begin after the first full year of employment or least after the initial introductory period is completed satisfactorily. Employees should notify supervisors of their birthday leave one month in advance, and they should identify the leave as such on their time sheet. The birthday leave is to be taken on the birthday or, if the birthday falls on a weekend or holiday, on the adjacent days within a week of the birthday. The nonprofit organization should reserve the right to require employees to work on their birthday if leave on that day poses a hardship to the organization. In such cases, the birthday leave should be granted at the earliest convenient time and no later than 30 days past the birthday.

EMPLOYEE DISCOUNTED PRODUCTS AND/OR SERVICES

Rationale

Nonprofits may wish to consider negotiating with other nonprofits for discounted products and services. This may be done through a barter arrangement. For example, a nonprofit that offers training programs could provide free or discounted staff training in return for child or elder care at a reduced rate or tickets to arts and cultural events. Also, for-profit businesses may provide discounts to nonprofits as a part of their community relations or marketing programs.

COMMUTING SUBSIDY

Rationale

Cost of commuting can be high and can create barriers to recruitment and retention of staff. A commuting subsidy is a cash benefit. Nonprofits will need to weigh the cost benefit carefully. The benefit may be paid parking, public transportation passes, or mileage reimbursement. The policy should be in writing. Requests for reimbursement of commuting expenses on a standard form provides the basis for reimbursement.

MISCELLANEOUS LEAVE

BEREAVEMENT LEAVE

Rationale

Bereavement leave policies provide staff persons with a specified number of days off following the death of an immediate family member. Immediate family is defined as spouse or life partner in the case of gay and lesbian staff, mother or father, sisters and brothers, and children, including step and adoptive relationships. Five days' leave is common for immediate family with reduction to three days off for more extended family including grandmothers and grandfathers, in-laws, aunts and uncles. In cases in which the more extended family was functioning as the employee's immediate family, the organization can grant longer leave. The bereaved employee should notify the supervisor immediately of the death in the family and receive verbal approval for the leave to be followed by written documentation by the supervisor. The employee then will record the leave on the time sheets as bereavement leave.

UNIFORMED SERVICES EMPLOYMENT AND REEMPLOYMENT RIGHTS

Rationale

Under a federal law called USERRA (Uniformed Services Employment and Reemployment Rights Act), employers have certain obligations with regard to reemployment, salary, health benefits, accrual of vacation and sick days, pension plans, and more. The Department of Labor expects employers to comply with this law. State statutes also may deal with employee uniformed services employment and reemployment rights.

FEDERAL LAWS

Veterans Reemployment Rights Act:

The Veterans Reemployment Rights Act of 1948 (38 USC 2021) requires that an employer must grant at least unpaid leave (with or without pay is up to the employer) to an employee who is called to leave a full time position for active military duty.

Within 90 days of when the employee has completed his or her military obligations (or after not more than one year of hospitalization after discharge from active duty), the employer shall reinstate the employee to their former position or to a position of like seniority, status, and pay.

Should that employee be unable to perform the duties of their original position due to a disability suffered during their military service, the employer must still offer the employee a position that the veteran can perform in, and which carries approximately the same seniority, status, and pay of the previously held position.

This law means that returning veterans have the right to "bump" out any persons who were hired to replace them in their absence.

This law applies to all who are called to duty, including military reservists and National Guard members.

Continuation of Health Benefits Under COBRA

Under the provisions of the Consolidated Omnibus Budget Reconciliation Act (COBRA) of 1985, any and all health insurance coverage provided to employees and dependents (if offered) must be continued for a period of 18 months after call-up of the employee if the employee or dependent receiving the coverage elects to do so within 60 days of the date of the call to duty.

Payment of the health premium is still the responsibility of the employee if that was the original arrangement.[12]

JURY DUTY AND SUBPOENAED LEAVE

Rationale

Employers must offer employees leave for jury duty or to respond to subpoenas. In the case of jury duty, the staff person may receive compensation for jury duty. The nonprofit may wish to continue the employee's pay as usual or may wish to deduct from the pay the amount the employee is paid for jury service. Normal pay usually is continued for leave to respond to a subpoena with reduction for any amount the staff person is compensated for answering the subpoena.

If a staff person or his or her family is a crime victim, the person also may have to appear in court and take time away from work. Time often is charged against annual leave or, as circumstances warrant, as sick time or considered leave without pay.

Staff members should notify their supervisors as soon as possible about the need for this type of leave. Documents should be required to verify the jury service or subpoena response time or witness fees, if any. Upon verification from court personnel (i.e., letter from prosecutor/attorney, etc.), victims of a crime may submit a written request for "court attendance" to their immediate supervisor. The supervisor and executive director must approve the request. Time off will be charged to accrued vacation time or time off without pay. Staff members must provide verification of attendance from court personnel.

LEAVE OF ABSENCE WITHOUT PAY

Rationale

Nonprofits that are not large enough to be covered by the Family and Medical Leave Act will want to establish a leave without pay policy. The FMLA can provide a model for small nonprofits. They may wish to adopt a policy providing similar benefits for covered types of leave even though technically they are not required to do so. Such a policy also should cover leave without pay unrelated to the FMLA. The policy should include the maximum length of time available and the conditions for the employee's return, including job reinstatement. A requirement might be that any applicable accrued leave the employee has earned should be used prior to being granted leave without pay. Insurance benefits may continue depending on the policies' terms and subject to state laws, but the staff person may be asked to pay the premiums for the leave period. If the nonprofit pays the insurance premium, the policy should require the staff person to reimburse the nonprofit for any benefits paid during leave. No leave benefits are accrued during the leave without pay.

Voting Leave

Rationale

Voting is a duty and a right for all citizens. It is in keeping with the values of the nonprofit sector, sometimes referred to as civil society, to adopt policies that make it easy for employees to vote. Adopting a policy for time off or flexible schedules for election days is an easy way to encourage voting.

Educational Leave

Rationale

Employee performance will be enhanced through participation in job-related training and education. During the employee's performance appraisal, training and education needs should be identified. The employee may find the right opportunity, or the employer may select and provide the training needed to enhance job performance. Career growth is another valid reason for providing training or education aimed at in-house promotion of a valued employee. Sometimes the training is for groups of employees to address an identified need they have in common.

The key is to be sure there is a tie between organization and employee performance and that the training is aligned to produce an identifiable result. When this is the case, the nonprofit's investment in training is wise. Funds should be dedicated in support of training and education each year. Supervisors should approve the training.

Other

Relocation

Rationale

When a nonprofit recruits staff from outside the community, the issue of reimbursement for relocation expenses most likely will come up. A relocation policy is an excellent recruiting tool, removing a part of the financial barrier to accepting the position. However, the nonprofit must examine its budget to determine what it can afford beyond the salary and standard benefits provided. If this is an unusual occurrence, it may be best to handle it on a case-by-case basis. If a policy is developed, it should be stated in terms of reimbursement for specific expenses such as payment of movers or payment for van rental and mileage. The nonprofit should qualify the policy by stating that such reimbursement will be available if the budget is adequate.

Reimbursement terms for moving expenses are handled as part of the hiring process. The executive director should approve the terms of all hires, including relocation reimbursement. If the hire is the executive director, the board president should approve the relocation terms. The nonprofit may ask the new recruit to obtain competitive bids for moving services and justify why one was selected over the others. Copies of contracts and receipts must be submitted for reimbursement to be given. If mileage is reimbursed, the nonprofit should do so at the rate it usually offers.

PROFESSIONAL MEMBERSHIPS

Rationale

Employees at managerial and professional levels may wish to participate in membership in professional associations. If the professional association is well chosen, it can be very helpful for improvement of morale, development of skills, building useful networks, and keeping the employee up to date in the field. It is a benefit for both the employee and the employer. The employer usually pays the annual cost of membership and also may budget for meeting attendance if finances allow. The nonprofit should require approval by the supervisor prior to payment of dues.

QUALIFIED TRANSPORTATION BENEFIT

Rationale

The Transportation Equity Act for the 21st Century allows employers to offer a plan so employees who commute to work using certain types of public transportation can receive reimbursement for their costs that does not count as taxable income to the employee or for the purposes of employer match on payroll taxes. The IRS code Section 132(f) sets the limit on the amount of money an employee can use on a monthly basis for transportation expenses. For 2003, the limit was $100 per month for mass transit expenses or up to $190 a month for costs associated with parking. Both types of expenses can be elected if qualified. The IRS may change the amounts annually. The net effect for the employee is discounted transportation expenses.

These areas qualify for transportation fringe benefits. The organization may provide an employee with any one or more of these benefits simultaneously.

- Transportation in a commuter highway vehicle is transportation provided by an organization to an employee in connection with travel between the employee's residence and place of employment. A "commuter highway vehicle" is a highway vehicle with a seating capacity of at least 6 adults (excluding the driver) and with at least 80 percent of the vehicle's mileage reasonably expected to be for transporting employees in connection with travel between their residences and their place of employment; and on trips during which the number of employees transported for commuting is at least one-half of the adult seating capacity of the vehicle (excluding the driver).
- A transit pass is any pass, token, fare-card, voucher, or similar item (including an item exchangeable for fare media) that entitles a person to transportation on mass transit facilities (whether or not the transit facilities are publicly owned) or provided by any person in the business of transporting persons for compensation or hire in a highway vehicle with a seating capacity of at least 6 adults (excluding the driver).
- Qualified parking is parking provided to an employee by the nonprofit on or near the nonprofit's business premises; or at a location from which the employee commutes to work by carpool, commuter highway vehicle, mass transit facilities, transportation provided by any person in the business of transporting persons for compensation or hire by any other means.[13]

INNOVATIVE COMPENSATION

Bonuses and Other Incentive Pay

Rationale

Bonuses are awards paid at senior management's discretion to acknowledge outstanding individual job performance or to encourage special activities. Bonuses usually are paid at the managerial levels and the amount is discretionary as it is not based on a predetermined formula. Use of bonuses as a part of total compensation is very common in for-profit companies. Nonprofits may mistakenly believe they cannot offer bonuses or other supplemental pay. The IRS Counsel Memorandum 38283, Revenue Ruling 8122068 1980, specifically removed prohibitions against the use of profit-sharing incentive pay systems in nonprofit organizations. Nonprofits are increasingly offering bonuses. The Nonprofit Times Salary Survey, 2003, reported that 13 percent of the respondents offered chief executive officer performance-based bonuses with average amounts equaling 8.7 percent.[14]

Nonprofits may wish to include the policy about bonuses in their overall compensation policy. The bonus policy should state who is eligible, how the bonus is earned, and by whom it is administered. Bonuses usually are awarded annually. Factors that influence bonus earnings include employee performance, the financial state of the nonprofit, and how bonuses factor into the overall compensation policy of the organization.

Other forms of incentive pay include:

- *Individual incentives.* These are cash awards to recognize achievement of predetermined performance objectives. An incentive award usually is calculated as a percentage of salary or salary range midpoint and is paid on an annual basis. Incentive awards usually are larger than spot awards and are used frequently at the managerial level.

- *Team or group incentives.* These are the same as individual incentives, except awards are based on a team or group's achievement of predetermined performance objectives.

- *Gain sharing.* These awards represent the employees' share of the gains of actual results achieved against preestablished operational goals. When the goals are exceeded, the "gains" are paid in the form of short-term cash incentive awards.

- *Spot awards.* These cash payments provide immediate recognition of accomplishments by staff below the managerial level. They are intended to reward risk taking, creativity, and productivity. Awards usually are paid immediately after the accomplishment and are separate from the regular salary administration program. Spot awards can recognize both individual and team achievements. These are generally smaller amounts of money than bonuses.

- *Special cash recognition.* These cash awards are used to recognize contributions of staff below a specified managerial level. They usually are granted on a discretionary basis to employees who demonstrate exceptional sustained or one-time effort performance. They can be of any amount but are often smaller than bonuses but somewhat larger than spot awards. They can be paid anytime or quarterly.

- *Special noncash recognition.* These are awards used to recognize contributions of staff, especially below management level. These may be merchandise, a gift certificate, and the like.

- *Lump sum increases.* Cash payments are made in a single lump sum to recognize performance achievements. They are not added to the base salary. They may replace a more traditional merit increase that is in the form of an adjustment in base pay.

- *Skill-based pay/pay for knowledge.* This pay is given to reward acquisition of additional job-related skills and capabilities.[15]

Employee Referral Bonus

Rationale

To aid a nonprofit in recruiting quality personnel, a bonus may be available to a current employee who refers an applicant who ultimately is hired. The idea is that existing employees know the organization and its culture well. They have networks they can access, and the promise of a bonus creates an incentive for them to do so. The policy should cover awards, their amount, and the procedure staff members must follow to refer job candidates. Executives and other senior managers generally are excluded, as it is part of their job to recruit and hire qualified personnel. Obviously, the tightness of the job market and the difficulty the nonprofit is experiencing will influence the need for this type of bonus policy.

Staff Service Awards

Rationale

This policy is for recognition of long-term service to the nonprofit organization. Five years of quality service could be the place to start with five-year increments after the first milestone. These awards often are given at a group event and may be covered in organization newsletters. They may include a certificate, gift, or cash, or all of these. Such awards are one tool to encourage employees to stay and to decrease turnover. As required by law, federal and state taxes are deducted from cash awards.

REFERENCES

1. U.S. Department of Labor, Employment Standards Administration, Wage and Hour Division, "Executive, Administrative, Professional and Outside Sales Exemptions Under the Fair Labor Standards Act."
2. University of Denver, Department of Human Resources, 2199 S. University Boulevard, Denver, CO 80208.
3. U.S. Department of Labor, Washington, DC, www.dol.gov/dol//topic/health-plans/portability.htm.
4. U.S. Department of Labor, Washington, DC, www.dol.gov/dol/topic/health-plans/index.htm.
5. Ibid.
6. Ibid.
7. U.S. Department of Labor, Washington, DC, www.dol.gov/esa/whd/fmla/.
8. Information on workers' compensation laws is provided by Patrick Spencer, Managing Partner, Spencer & Spencer, P.C., 830 Tenderfoot Hill Road, Suite 320, Colorado Springs, CO 80809, 719-632-4808.
9. Joan E. Pynes, *Human Resources Management for Public and Nonprofit Organizations*, (San Francisco: Jossey-Bass, John Wiley & Sons, Inc., 1997). www.josseybass.com
10. U.S. Department of Labor, Washington, DC, www.dol.gov/esa/whd/fmla/.
11. U.S. Department of Labor, Employment Standards Administration, Wage and Hour Division, Family and Medical Leave Act of 1993, Washington, DC
12. U.S. Department of Labor, Veteran's Employment and Training Service, 401 S. State Street, Two North, Chicago, IL 60605.
13. U.S. Department of Transportation, Washington, DC, www.house.gov/transportation/highway/issues/tea21/sum.htm.
14. *The Nonprofit Times*, February 2003, Parsippany, New Jersey.
15. Carol L. Barbeito and Jack P. Bowman, *Nonprofit Compensation and Benefits Practices* (New York: John Wiley & Sons, Inc., 1998).

CHAPTER 5

Supervision

This chapter offers some policies that may be helpful in regard to supervision of staff persons.

PERFORMANCE APPRAISALS

Rationale

Performance appraisals are an important part of a human resource management system. Hiring the first employee signals the need for adoption of a process for performance reviews. The appraisals may be done at the completion of the initial period of employment and at least at annual intervals. They should not be the only feedback system. Supervisors should have an ongoing dialogue with employees on their performance and receive input from employees about how the supervisor and the organization can support them. However, after the initial employment period, a formal review usually is done at the end of the noprofit's official year.

The basis for the evaluation should be the job description, goals, performance standards, previous performance goals for that employee, and any special issues the employee was working on to improve performance. It is very important that all parties know the criteria and process in advance. The performance process should be well documented. It should include a two-way discussion between the employee and the supervisor. The contents of the review should be confidential except when there are higher-level managers who need to provide input or at least be informed about employees' performance.

The appraisal becomes a part of the employment record and file for each employee. Appraisals should be signed and dated by both the employee and the supervisor conducting the appraisal. In the event the appraisal is in dispute, the employee may not sign; in this case, the supervisor should note that fact on the record and ask the employee to provide a written statement as to what he or she disagrees with and why he or she will not sign the appraisal. The lack of signature does not negate the appraisal, and the organization should expect the employee to address any performance deficits.

The purpose of appraisals is to identify and acknowledge performance strengths and to identify areas of performance that need to be improved. They also provide employees with an opportunity to give their supervisor input regarding what they feel they need to achieve better performance. Training needs, equipment needs, more time with the supervisor, and more or improved information are some of the resources an employee might bring to the supervisor's attention.

Performance appraisals are used as the basis for identification of employee performance goals for the next year and relate to compensation decisions as well as transfer, promotion, demotion, and termination decisions.

DISCIPLINARY POLICIES

Rationale

The organization should have a policy that states what the steps in disciplinary action are. This policy should be part of the orientation of all employees. Verbal warnings are often the first step in disciplinary action. Verbal warnings are less formal than written warnings. The supervisor may or may not wish to make a note in the employee's personnel record about the warning, but should make an informal note about the conversation for his or her own reference. If the problem persists, it will be very helpful to be able to document the effort made to address the problem through verbal warning. Formal, written warnings that identify and detail the problem and list expectations for improvement and disciplinary measures that will occur if the problem is not corrected are part of the permanent record. A supervisor and the staff person should sign written warnings, and a signed copy should be placed in the staff person's personnel file.

Actions that might be taken if the problem is not resolved may include demotion, no merit increase, or termination. Of course, in the event of malfeasance by the employee, it may be necessary to move to suspension or termination without the warning steps. All actions should be fully documented, including description of the problem, date, steps taken to allow the employee to correct the problem, what improvements still are needed, the period of time for corrections to occur, and what will happen if the problem is not corrected. The supervisor also should note how he or she will support the employee during the disciplinary and correction period.

If a staff person refuses to sign, the supervisor should note that on the documentation and ask the staff person to sign indicating refusal to sign the document. If this is refused, the supervisor may call on a superior manager to witness that a copy of the unsigned documentation was given to the staff person. The staff person's signature indicates receipt of the document, but not agreement with it.

DISMISSAL

Rationale

Dismissal may occur as the last step in a progressive disciplinary action, for continuing inability to meet job performance standards or when a staff member commits a serious offense. Personnel policies should identify the types of offenses that are considered serious and are grounds for immediate dismissal. Examples of such offenses are using or selling drugs or alcohol on the job, assault of another person on the job, bringing weapons to work, or theft.

An at-will employer can dismiss a staff person at any time, for any reason. The state the nonprofit operates in may or may not recognize at-will employment. If the state does not recognize at-will employment, the nonprofit must prove just cause for dismissing an employee. Documentation of the progressive discipline, unsatisfactory performance, or serious offense is critical. The documentation should be placed in the employee's personnel file, and such files should be secured.

LAYOFFS

Rationale

Nonprofits may face situations requiring a reduction of staff. A layoff policy may be adopted as needed, or the organization may wish to develop one as a contingency. The policy should specify the notice period prior to laying off an employee and how long salary and benefits will be continued. Annual leave earned must be paid along with the final salary. Nonprofits should take care to avoid discrimination against protected classes when they select those employees to be laid off. Organizations may wish to state methods they will use to achieve the needed staffing reductions. Those methods might include:

- Voluntary reductions in the workforce, including staff members who take early retirement, leaves of absence, or reductions in hours
- Attrition
- Termination of part-time positions prior to termination of full-time positions
- Transfers of staff to other vacant positions

The notice of layoffs should come from the executive director and should provide the reasons for the layoff, what means are being used to achieve the staff reduction, the notice period, and what recourse (if any) is available to staff members being laid off.

GRIEVANCE PROCEDURE

Rationale

A grievance procedure should be included in the personnel policies that are given to all staff members upon hire and when policy changes are made. One element of the policy is the chain of command. Staff members must know whom to take grievances to first; usually it is the immediate supervisor. In rare instances, a staff person might be allowed to bypass the supervisor, as when the complaint is about harassment by the supervisor. If the nonprofit has a human resource department, it may become involved if the staff person's supervisor does not satisfy the grievance. The executive director is the final step in terms of staff. Finally, the board of directors is the court of last appeal in terms of internal action on the grievance. The board may wish to form an ad hoc committee appointed by the president, or a regular committee, such as the executive committee, may be responsible.

The procedure for filing a grievance should require staff persons to state their grievance in writing. The policy should state time lines for action the employee takes and the responses for each step in the process. It also should state that those filing complaints would not be penalized in any way.

Grievances should be limited to terms of employment as defined in the personnel policies and contracts if any, compensation, benefits, discrimination, promotions, transfers, and termination. Grievances are not about personality conflicts.

CHAPTER 6

Employment Conditions

This chapter offers policies that relate to the personal conduct of employees, employer administration, and support for employees.

EMPLOYMENT CONFLICT OF INTEREST

Rationale

A conflict of interest may occur when an employee is working outside of the organization for a competitor on a paid or volunteer basis. The nonprofit may wish to allow outside employment but may require staff members to disclose their other work and have written agreement from their supervisor. This protects both the employer and the employee from future misunderstandings. The employer will be able to determine in advance if the outside job will interfere with the employment in the nonprofit and if a conflict of interest is present. The employee will be able to take the outside work secure in the knowledge that it will not conflict with employment in the nonprofit. Staff members who are on medical or family leave are not eligible for outside employment during the time of their leave.

Another source of conflict is when employees accept gifts or special favors from anyone who uses or might use the nonprofit's services. The conflict may arise if the service provider thinks the employee owes them a favor in return.

GOVERNMENT, POLITICAL ACTIVITY, PERSONAL BELIEFS, AND VALUES

Rationale

It is important that employees' political opinions and religious and other personal beliefs or values are not mistaken for the opinions and beliefs of the nonprofit organization. This does not preclude the right of any person to have opinions and beliefs and to express them as individuals. Employees should not be allowed to coerce others involved with the nonprofit about their beliefs, and care should be taken that employees never leave the impression they are speaking on behalf of the nonprofit they work for when expressing their personal opinions.

Staff members who wish to seek elective office should inform their supervisors and the executive director. Subject to the requirements of law and the leave policies of the organization, unpaid personal leave may be granted for the purposes of campaigning.

DRUG-FREE WORKPLACE

Rationale

The Drug-Free Workplace Act became federal law in 1989. It requires all federal government contractors and grant recipients of $25,000 to certify that they are providing a drug-free work environment. To qualify as a drug-free workplace, an employer must:

- Notify employees by published statement that the unlawful manufacture, distribution, dispensation, possession, or use of a controlled substance is prohibited in the workplace. The statement must specify actions that will be taken against violators. Employees working on the grant or contract must receive a copy of the statement.
- Include compliance with the statement and employer notification within five days of any criminal drug conviction that occurs in the workplace.
- Tell workers that they must notify their employer if they are convicted of any workplace drug crime within ten days of notice of conviction.

- Establish a drug-free awareness campaign program to tell workers about drug counseling programs, and the program must cover: dangers of drug use, employer's workplace drug policy, information on drug counseling, rehabilitation, employee assistance programs, and penalties for drug abuse violations in the workplace.

- Require satisfactory participation in a drug abuse, assistance, or rehabilitation program by any employee with a workplace drug conviction or impose a sanction.

- Implement all of the above as a good faith effort to maintain a drug-free workplace.

Should the nonprofit fail to comply or if it is determined by U.S. Government OMB that the nonprofit has not made a good faith effort, penalties include suspension or disbarment which means that the employer becomes ineligible for future grants and contracts for a period not to exceed five years.[1] Contact OMB Financial Management Division at 202-395-3053 for grants. For contracts, contact OMB, Office of Federal Procurement Policy at 202-395-3300.

Smoking

Rationale

State and local laws governing smoking will provide nonprofits with the legal framework that affects their own policies. Smoke-free work environments are very common, and adopting a policy that clarifies the nonprofit's position to limit smoking to certain designated areas either within the building or outside is wise.

Policy

This nonprofit provides a smoke-free work environment and is in compliance with state and local laws regarding smoking in the workplace. No smoking is allowed inside or outside the building except in designated areas outside the building. Smokers are responsible for keeping the area free of litter. Violation of this policy will result in disciplinary action.

Telephone Calls

Rationale

Use of the telephone at work should be for business use primarily, and a policy that states this is useful. Staff members will need to make local calls to coordinate with family and friends and sometimes to handle their own personal business that must be done during their work hours. When frequency of personal calls or length of such calls interferes with the employee's productivity, the supervisor will need to take action. The supervisor's enforcement of the use of the phone is helped by a policy that states that personal calls should be made on breaks when possible and, when personal calls must be made or taken during active work hours, should be kept short.

Employees who need to make long-distance calls at work should charge them to a telephone credit card or their home phone. If they must make a long-distance call from a business phone, a call log should be created with the number called, date, time, and name of employee. Employees will be required to reimburse the nonprofit for any long-distance personal calls they make from the business phone.

Code of Ethics

Rationale

Many organizations are adopting codes of ethics that cover all persons working as paid staff or volunteers, including the board. A code of ethics provides operating instructions for the organization's values. Developing a code of ethics involves getting a commitment from all key stakeholders, discussions among stakeholder representatives, writing the code, board approval, and implementation. All persons working on behalf of the nonprofit should receive a copy of the code of ethics as a part of their orientation. The code of ethics formally states the nonprofit's commitment to high standards of ethical behavior. The code should be actively utilized throughout the organization.

Change of Personal Information

Rationale

Staff members should notify their employer in writing within a week of when their names, addresses, phone numbers, e-mails, or contacts to call in an emergency change, as these changes can affect their pay and benefits.

Staff Identification Cards

Rationale

In larger organizations or when access to the workplace is controlled and for security concerns, staff identification cards may be issued. These cards will aid receptionists and security personnel as well as the other staff members to verify identity and check for approved access. Access may be different for different staff members, depending on the nature of the mission of the nonprofit and the need to secure certain materials, such as personnel files and fund-raising records. The policy should state whether a picture is required and how it is obtained, who authorizes the card, and the level of access for the employee. Upon termination or suspension, employees should be required to turn their identification card over to their supervisor or the human resource department immediately. Access permissions with receptionists and security should then exclude those persons from the authorized list.

Travel

Rationale

A travel policy that describes what expenses are covered at what rate when employees travel helps the organization better estimate costs and control costs. It provides a uniform guideline so staff persons know in advance how their travel will be paid for and at what terms. The travel policy should include: air travel class, automobile mileage reimbursement, tolls, gas for rental car, car rental, taxis, shuttles, hotel rating, per diem allowed for meals, and what other costs will be covered such as phone calls home. The policy should state whether travel advances are available, for what, and how they can be obtained. It also should state the procedures employees must follow to be reimbursed. Sometimes nonprofits require travel to be centrally arranged for control or discounting purposes. If so, that fact should be part of the policy. Staff members may have travel discounts and special upgrade arrangements they have obtained personally. It is common to allow employees to keep points earned for travel for the business for personal use. Sometimes staff members can obtain equal or better rates and accommodations for travel by using their own upgrade or discount coupons. This can make business travel more comfortable, and it seems wise to allow it as long as it does not cost the nonprofit more money.

Policy

Staff members may be required to travel on behalf of this organization and as a part of their job. They are entitled to reimbursement for expenses incurred while on business travel as follows:

- Economy air fare, booked as far in advance as possible
- Car rental for medium-size car unless the travel involves unusual conditions
- Three-star hotels
- Gas at actual prices
- Mileage at rate established by the IRS
- Taxis, tolls at actual
- Standard per diem for meals $50 per day

Receipts must be presented along with a signed travel reimbursement request to the supervisor. Travel advances are only available with executive director approval when a financial hardship exists for the employee who is going to travel.

TIME CLOCK

Rationale

Certain types of nonprofits may use a time clock as a method of recording the hours worked by nonexempt staff. This method helps track the number of hours worked to avoid overtime. When pay is based on actual hours worked, it provides an accurate record. The policy regarding time clocks should state that each staff person must use the time clock him- or herself and that checking in or out for another staff person is a serious violation.

WORK SCHEDULES

Rationale

Personnel policies may state the hours the organization office is open, and staff work schedules may conform to the standard hours of business. However, this is not necessarily the case. Service workers may have alternative schedules because of client needs or due to covering shifts. At times exempt staff schedules may require long hours and evening and weekend work.

Flex time is increasingly popular, allowing employees whose work does not require them to be at a set location on a regular schedule to adopt more flexible schedules. This benefit to employees may help them balance personal demands, reduce commuting time, and sometimes be more productive.

When employees are recruited, work schedule expectations for the position they are applying for should be discussed to avoid a mismatch of expectations.

Employer Administration and Support for Employees

Personnel Records

Rationale

Documentation from the employment application through the hiring agreement and for the full term of employment for every employee is essential. Files should be organized carefully and kept up to date. Care should be taken that notes and additions to the file are written in a professional manner. In most states, employees have the right to review their file. Should there ever be dispute, the contents of personnel files may be the basis for ruling on the dispute. Files should be kept in a secure area, and no one should have access to them except authorized personnel. If an employee asks to review his or her file, this should be done in a designated area while the person authorized to maintain the files is present. Employees may not remove items from their files. They may copy items from their files. Employees should request review of their files in writing. Response to these requests should be within 10 days.

Policy

Employee personnel files are confidential. The only persons with access to the file shall be the employee, his or her immediate supervisor, and others higher up in the chain of command, such as department head and executive director.

Staff personnel files contain these items:

- Application and resume
- Letters of appointment and acceptance
- Job description

- Copies of transcripts, diplomas, certificates, and licenses
- Ongoing performance evaluations
- Documents relating to performance
- Documentation of job changes or transfers
- Training records
- Leave of absence information
- Signed code of ethics
- Documentation required by state or private regulatory agencies

TELECOMMUTING

Rationale

Advances in technology have created the opportunity for employees to conduct their work from home or various distance locations. This can be a major plus, eliminating commuting costs and time and allowing blocks of work that fit personal schedules. Telecommuting can be a recruitment and retention incentive. Expectations regarding the workplace should be part of hiring and promotion agreements; however, the employer should retain the right to change workplaces as needed. Some problems can be loss of face-to-face time with other employees and supervisors. Organizations will want to consider how to create a sense of belonging and connection when adopting telecommuting policies.

Unions should be consulted to make sure the policy does not violate collective bargaining agreements. Not all positions can be performed through telecommuting so care must be taken when adopting a policy to ensure that staff persons do not consider it an entitlement. Another factor to be considered is if employees have the skill level, experience, and personal maturity to succeed at their job if telecommuting. Jobs need to be structured and clear outputs and outcomes identified.

CREDIT CARDS

Rationale

The organization may wish to issue credit cards for selected employees (see Exhibit 6.1). The executive director may have one, as people in such positions often have to travel and/or entertain others as a part of their job. Company credit cards can be an efficient arrangement that is beneficial to employees, as they do not have to pay expenses of the nonprofit from their personal funds. Employers are permitted to do a credit check on job applicants and staff members, this should be done before a credit card is issued. The credit card policy should state that the credit record of staff members to whom a credit card is being issued will be checked. Staff members should sign a memo stating they have been advised that such a credit check will be done. They should know that they can check their rights under the Fair Credit Reporting Act and other applicable laws. The credit card is the property of the nonprofit; the employee it is issued to is the signer and dedicated user. All usual accounting procedures regarding documentation of expenses should apply to the payment of the credit card bills. Other policies regarding employee expense reimbursement also apply. Credit cards must be surrendered at the time of separation from the organization. Care should be taken to have the authorized signer of the card changed immediately.

Policy

EXHIBIT 6.1	CREDIT CARD REQUEST

Name: _____ Job Title: _____
              (Please Print)

Employee Number: _____

Type of Card Requested

		Date		Date
		Card Issued	Number	Card Returned
_____	Car Rental (Hertz)	_____	_____	_____
_____	Air Travel (TWA)	_____	_____	_____
_____	Telephone (C&P)	_____	_____	_____
_____	Credit	_____	_____	_____

Cardholder's Signature: _____ Date: _____

Authorized Approval: _____ Date: _____

CREDIT BACKGROUND CHECKS

Rationale

The law permits an employer to conduct an investigation into the credit background of staff members or job applicants. A policy about this should state that staff members or job applicants whose backgrounds will be checked will be notified and that they can learn of their credit report under the Fair Credit Reporting Act. Staff persons should be asked to sign a statement that they have been informed about the check and their rights.

COLLECTIVE BARGAINING

Rationale

Collective bargaining is defined as a process that obligates management and union representatives to negotiate in good faith in an attempt to reach an agreement concerning issues that affect employees. Tests for the law's coverage include interstate flow of money or goods and annual income, plus type of business the nonprofit offers. Health care, for example, was added in 1974. In 1979 the Supreme Court ruled that the National Labor Relations Board does not have jurisdiction over church-operated schools, but it does have jurisdiction over church-related hospitals and child care centers. Nonprofit service organizations that provide services to or for an exempt governmental agency that is supported by state and/or federal funds are included. State law on this subject varies.

Each organization should know whether it is within the jurisdiction of the National Labor Relations Board or not.

REFERENCE

1. OMB Financial Management Division, 10225 New Executive Office Building, OMB, Washington, DC, 20503 and OMB, Office of Federal Procurement Policy, 9025 New Executive Office Building, Washington, DC, 20503.

CHAPTER 7

Administration

This chapter includes policies related to use of organization assets, real and intellectual; policies related to safety, security and health; and office management policies.

USE OF ORGANIZATION ASSETS

USE OF NONPROFIT ASSETS IN THE PUBLIC POLICY PROCESS

Rationale

Following a long effort by a large and diverse group of public charities from 1970 to 1990, the IRS published final lobbying regulations for charities designed as section 501(c)(3) of the IRS Code. The legislation enacted in 1976 added sections 501(h) and 4911 to the IRS Code. Nonprofits can elect to be governed by the 501(h) and 4911 rules and all charities are subject to the 501(c)(3) rules. Under the 501(c)(3) code there is a statement that charities may not attempt to influence legislation as a "substantial part" of their activities. The "new" rules make most charities eligible to elect; which makes lobbying expenditures the sole test of the permissibility of lobbying and specify dollar allowances for a charity's lobbying expenditures. When the charity elects to be covered under the new rules, they [*sic*] are able to operate within the detailed and quite favorable definition of what does and does not constitute lobbying. The rules also create a system highly protective of private foundation grants to lobbying public charities. Public charities that are engaged in lobbying will find it in their interests to make the 501(h) election. These new rules do not apply to private foundations except in terms of grants they make to public charities or churches and their integrated auxiliaries.

More information can be obtained by accessing the Web site of Charity Lobbying in the Public Interest at www.clpi.org. For more information about 501(c)(3) organizations and political activities, contact the Internal Revenue Service.[1]

NONPROFIT VEHICLES

Rationale

When the nonprofit staff owns or rents vehicles that are driven by staff or volunteers, a policy regarding qualifications of drivers and use of the vehicles is needed. The policy should cover the kind of information that must be on file, what is required in reporting of moving violations, what the driving standards are, and what the consequences are for moving violations.

Policy

This policy affects any individual who may drive a nonprofit vehicle or personal vehicle on nonprofit business. Prior to driving a vehicle, this information must be in the employee's personnel file:

- A record check with the Bureau of Motor Vehicles and proof of absence of more than two moving violations for a three-year period
- Proof of insurance, if personal vehicles are used for nonprofit business

All information will be kept confidential. It is the staff member's responsibility to keep this information up-to-date, including reporting to the executive director any moving violations or changes in driving status within five days of the violation or change. Failure to do this can result in disciplinary action up to and including termination.

If a staff member accumulates more than two moving violations in any vehicle, personal or nonprofit, it will be up to the insurance carrier to decide if the staff member will lose driving privileges on nonprofit business for a period of up to three years. Any staff member committing a moving violation in a nonprofit vehicle or personal vehicle on nonprofit business also may be subject to disciplinary action. Some job classifications require a staff member to drive. Dismissal from these positions may occur if a staff member receives a moving violation in any vehicle.

Safe driving practices, speed limits, and other driving laws must be observed at all times. This nonprofit is not responsible for fines incurred by staff members while driving a nonprofit vehicle or a personal vehicle while on nonprofit business. Staff members are responsible for reporting any accidents, no matter how minor, to the police before leaving the scene of the accident and as soon as possible to the executive director.

Persons authorized to do business for the nonprofit and who attend meetings in other places are expected to use nonprofit vehicles. If there is no vehicle available, and the staff member has prior approval of the appropriate supervisor, personal vehicles may be used for nonprofit business. Mileage for staff travel on nonprofit business will be reimbursed at the rate recognized by the IRS for the current year. The reimbursed rate for 2004 is 0.375 per mile.

USE OF PERSONAL VEHICLES

Rationale

It is common for staff persons to use their personal vehicles for business purposes. Reimbursement of mileage is a common benefit. The rate of reimbursement can be set at any level, but the IRS establishes the rate it recognizes each year for tax deduction purposes, and this rate provides a good reference for the nonprofit. Most bookkeepers and accountants should be able to provide the current IRS rate. Staff members should keep a record of business travel while using their vehicle, reporting the date, destination, and number of miles. This record should be submitted in the same manner as all expense reimbursements are. The nonprofit will cover the mileage reimbursement at the rate adopted for the year.

PERSONAL PHOTOCOPYING AND FAX MACHINES

Rationale

Use of any of the nonprofit's property for personal use should be discouraged as that property was purchased with funds gained in support of the mission of the organization. There may be occasions when a staff person has a compelling need for a small number of copies or to send a fax. A control procedure should be in place in which an administrator is designated to receive a request from the staff person indicating how many copies or faxes are needed and the date. The staff person then will be charged for those copies or faxes at a predetermined rate that fully covers the nonprofit's costs. The following policy can be modified easily to include faxes.

Policy

Employees are discouraged from using this nonprofit's photocopying equipment for personal use. If an employee needs to make personal copies, they will be required to pay 10 cents per copy for all copies over a five-page limit per day. A log sheet will be maintained near every copy machine in every office for documentation of the amount of personal use. On a monthly basis, the log sheet is to be given to the administrative director so that the cost of personal copies can be deducted from the employee's paycheck.[2]

BULLETIN BOARDS

Rationale

Bulletin boards are important communication tools for nonprofits. Some purposes are to post legal notices that employers are required to keep on display, provide safety information, notify employees of job openings and other company events. Staff members should know that they need to check bulletin boards regularly.

COPYRIGHT

Rationale

Any material written or produced by staff in the course of their employment duties are the nonprofit's exclusive intellectual property. These materials can include software, training materials, or any publications or materials that are used by the nonprofit to accomplish its mission. For more information, contact the U.S. Copyright Office, a department of the Library of Congress.[3]

Policy

Any materials developed by staff members in the course and scope of their employment is the property of the nonprofit organization. It is the policy of this nonprofit to copyright written material, photographs, drawings, prints, and other materials when reproduction by others would be detrimental to the organization.

ACCEPTABLE USE OF THE INTERNET

Rationale

State and federal law regulate use of the Internet and forbid certain practices, such as accessing information without authorization or causing a system to malfunction.

Staff members also can abuse the Internet by using language that is libelous, sexually offensive, or harassing, which can place a nonprofit at risk of a lawsuit. Other abuses can include using the Internet to campaign for a political campaign, thus possibly jeopardizing the nonprofit's tax-exempt status, or simply using it to play games or send private messages during work hours. Downloading of pornography is another abuse. The policy should clearly state that use of the Internet is for the purposes of nonprofit business only and that the nonprofit may monitor its use by staff members to ensure use for nonprofit purposes rather than personal purposes.

Policy

- Use of the Internet is for nonprofit business only, and this nonprofit may monitor members' use of the Internet to ensure that it is being used for the stated purpose only.

- Users must abide by all existing federal and state laws regarding electronic communication. This includes, but is not limited to, accessing information without authorization, giving passwords out, or causing a system to malfunction.

- No advertising for profit or campaigns for political office are allowed.

- Users must not use language that is abusive, profane, or sexually offensive.

- E-mail is not guaranteed to be private.

CELLULAR TELEPHONE PROCEDURES

Rationale

The organization may provide cellular phones to employees as a benefit. The phones remain the property of the nonprofit, which pays the bills. Staff members who receive phones should sign for them and should be aware of the terms and limits of the policy covering use of the phones, which would include at least: service areas accessible within basic service contract; rates and areas for out-of-range calling; the number of minutes available; and expectations as to limits on overages or out-of-range calls. Staff members should know what to do about phone or service problems. Upon termination, the staff person should immediately surrender the phone and get a signed receipt.

Policy

This nonprofit provides cellular telephones for staff members who are in positions that consistently take them away from the main agency facility. These staff members may be provided a cellular telephone for their use and will be asked to sign for receipt of the phone. At this time, the specifics of the calling plan will be provided.

Use is for agency-related business calls. Personal calls should be for essential use and kept to a minimum of minutes. If call records show a consistent overage in minutes and use of the phone for personal calls that contributes to the overage, the staff person may be charged for the amount of personal minutes that contribute to the overage. The administrator should be contacted in the event the staff person cannot resolve phone or calling service problems.

Upon termination, the phone must be returned immediately and the staff person will be issued a receipt showing the return of the phone.

PAGER GUIDELINES

Rationale

For staff persons who are on call and who may need to be reached quickly, a pager may be issued. The pagers belong to the organization and are signed out to the staff. The staff person should know how the pager works and what to do in the case of problems. Upon termination, the staff person should turn the pager in and be given a signed receipt.

Policy

Please note the following concerning the use of the pager assigned to you:

1. During the hours of 7 A.M. to 9 P.M., please carry your pager with you. Even if you are not on the clock, an emergency may arise and we may need to contact you for your help or for vital information.

Another reason you may be paged prior to your scheduled "start time" is if there is a change in your schedule.

2. Please replace the battery as soon as you receive a "low cell" message. There are batteries in the office supply room.

3. Because there are many different reasons for someone to be paged, please note the following codes that will be used:

    • If the paged message has an extension from 3001 to 3021, call at your earliest convenience. The message is not an emergency. If you are at a location where there isn't a phone nearby or you are in the middle of an activity that would be difficult to interrupt, call in when you leave that location or complete that activity.

    • 555 means there is a schedule change. Call the office immediately. If you are traveling to a destination, please stop and use the nearest phone.

    • If an extension number is followed by 911, there is an emergency in progress. Call the office immediately.

    • The last code is 000. If you have been involved in a situation, for example, searching for a lost person, assisting with behavior support, it means "relax . . . all is fine now."[4]

SAFETY, SECURITY, AND HEALTH

INCLEMENT WEATHER AND EMERGENCY CLOSINGS

Rationale

It is helpful to have a policy and a communication system to cover emergency situations. The policy should cover who determines the weather or other emergency and declares the actions to be taken. Staff persons should be clear as to how they will be contacted or actions they need to take. Pay usually continues throughout emergency closings.

Policy

The executive director or the executive director's designee may close the nonprofit due to inclement weather or other emergencies when these days fall on regular workdays. A phone calling system and e-mail system will be activated and public media announcements will be made when possible.

Staff members should be proactive in checking for closing notices by checking phone messages, e-mails, and listening to media announcements during weather or other emergencies. Staff members also should contact their supervisor if unsure what to do about going to work.

The absence will be considered an excused absence for all staff members, and will not be charged to earned leave time. Should an emergency closing occur while a staff member is already on earned leave time, such as sick, vacation, or personal, the absence will be covered by the original leave purpose.

SAFETY STANDARDS AND EMERGENCY PROCEDURES

Rationale

The nonprofit will want to place emphasis on safety and prevention of accidents and emergencies. Policies regarding safety and emergencies should be posted on bulletin boards, provided in writing to all employees, and periodically reviewed with staff persons. It is a good idea for anyone working for the nonprofit, including volunteers and contractors at its facilities, to know what the procedures are and where they are posted. The Office of Homeland Security is a new source for information regarding national security concerns at www.homeland-directory.com. The Occupational and Safety and Health Administration (OSHA) is a good source for workplace safety information; check its Web site www.osha.gov. Another useful Web site is www.ready.gov.

ELECTRONIC MONITORING

Rationale

A nonprofit may want to monitor e-mails and can legally do so under limited conditions. The Federal Electronic Communications Privacy Act of 1986 prohibits the intentional interception of any type of electronic transmission, e-mail included, unless the employer has the consent of both communicating parties. The business extension of this act clearly allows businesses to monitor electronic communication in the normal course of business. Intentional interception is defined as preventing a message from getting through to its intended receiver. Monitoring transmission, however, only involves the employer determining whether the system is being used for work-related communication. Once the message is determined to be work-related or personal, the monitoring must discontinue.

If a policy is developed about monitoring e-mails, have staff members sign to acknowledge they have been informed of the policy when they are hired and include it in every staff persons' policy manual. This statement should be worded so it constitutes a warning that monitoring may occur.

EXPOSURE TO BODILY FLUIDS

Rationale

Procedures should be in place to help protect all persons at the organization from the risks of transmission of communicable diseases. A policy on exposure to bodily fluids should spell out rules and procedures that need to be followed when handling, cleaning up, and disposing of bodily fluids as well as cleaning clothing worn while working with them. The term "body fluids" applies to blood, drainage from scrapes and cuts, feces, urine, vomit, saliva, and drainage from any orifice. Besides the protection these procedures offer to the individuals involved, they may protect the organization from legal action. Exact recommended procedures can be found through the Occupational and Safety and Health Administration's (OSHA's) Web site, www.osha.org.

PROTECTIVE EQUIPMENT

Rationale

A policy that requires staff members to wear protective equipment when working in areas or performing job functions of concern is wise. The protective equipment is not an option, and staff members should be aware that they will be required to comply. In addition to protecting staff persons, such a policy may help keep workers' compensation premiums down and protects against legal fees and settlements. The policy should be stated in general terms rather than listing specific protective equipment and dangerous work areas.

SEAT BELTS

Rationale

In most states, laws require drivers and passengers in automobiles to wear seat belts. Seat belts save lives and prevent injuries. A policy requiring them to be used in all organization-owned vehicles, or when personal vehicles are used for business purposes, may be helpful to the nonprofit in the event of legal action. It may help lower insurance premiums also.

FIRE DRILLS

Rationale

The owner or manager of the building the nonprofit is in may conduct fire drills, or the nonprofit may, if it is the building owner or manager. Fire procedures should be posted on employee bulletin boards and known to all staff members. A fire drill puts those procedures to the test.

Policy

Fire drills may occur. All fire drills will be unannounced. Fire procedures are posted on all staff bulletin boards. Employees should familiarize themselves with fire procedures and emergency exits and will be required to participate in fire drills, which should be treated as the real thing.

HEPATITIS B VACCINATIONS

Rationale

Some nonprofit staff members have jobs that increase their risk of contracting hepatitis B. The nonprofit may wish to require staff members to be vaccinated against this highly contagious disease. The vaccinations should be provided as a no-cost benefit.

FIREARMS/WEAPONS

Rationale

A simple but strict policy on the possession of firearms and weapons in the workplace helps protect staff members, clients, and the public.

Policy

The possession of firearms or other dangerous weapons by employees of this nonprofit in the workplace is strictly forbidden. Any employee found to possess such items while on nonprofit property will be subject to immediate termination.

SOLICITATION AND DISTRIBUTION

Rationale

To help foster a productive environment, a nonprofit may wish to prohibit the solicitation and sale of goods on the premises. The solicitation policy should be posted at or near the entrance so solicitors are discouraged from entering.

IDENTITY THEFT

Rationale

Thieves are using identify data to steal money from individuals by assuming their identify. While outsiders may be involved, current and past employees may also. The nonprofit has the obligation to develop strong policies and procedures to protect the personal information you store on staff, volunteers, and clients.

Start by listing types of people you have information on such as paid staff, volunteers, service recipients, donors, etc. Know what information is collected, when and why. Document storage, who has access, and how privacy is protected. Look for the gaps and fix them. Create use policies and educate people about the policies and penalties for violation. Monitor policies to ensure compliance.[5]

REFERENCES

1. Charity Lobbying in the Public Interest, www.clpi.org.
2. Deaf Independent Living Association, Inc., PO Box 4038, 110 Baptist Street, Salisbury, MD 21803.
3. Copyright Office, Library of Congress, Washington, DC 20559-6000, http://lcweb.loc.gov/copyright.
4. CAPC, Inc., 7200 Greenleaf Avenue, Suite 170, Whittier, CA 90602-1363, www.capcinc.org.
5. The Nonprofit Risk Management Center, www.nonprofitrisk.com.

CHAPTER 8

Volunteer Policies

This chapter covers policies related to volunteer management that are part of human resource management as nonprofits utilize paid and unpaid workers to perform the functions of the organization.

ASSESSMENT OF VOLUNTEER MANAGEMENT SYSTEM

Rationale

Volunteers are valuable or even essential members of the workforce in many nonprofit organizations. To recruit, motivate, and retain volunteers requires the development of a volunteer management system within the organization's human resource management system. Results from the utilization of volunteers and the satisfaction of the volunteers will depend to a great extent on having a well-developed volunteer management system. The following assessment tool is an aid to understanding the components of the system and to planning for improvements.

Policy

Check those components of the volunteer management system that are in place in your agency, and then rate them for quality of development. Use this assessment (see Exhibit 8.1) to plan for further development of an effective and efficient system for managing volunteers.

EXHIBIT 8.1   VOLUNTEER MANAGEMENT ASSESSMENT TOOL

	Check One		Check Most Appropriate Level				
	Do Not Have:	Have:	Poor	Fair	Acceptable	Very Good	Excellent
1. Clear statement of organization mission							
2. Clear statement of long-term goals							
3. Analysis of numbers and types of volunteer resources needed							
4. Job descriptions for volunteer positions							
5. Recruitment plan for each type of volunteer							
6. Intake process							
7. Selection process							
8. Orientation and training							
9. Supervision							
10. Career development							
11. Recognition							
12. Record-keeping system							

Volunteer Application

Rationale

When a nonprofit determines that it will utilize volunteers, a job description should be developed and recruitment efforts will be used to reach out to potential qualified applicants. The nonprofit is in effect "hiring" the volunteer whose experience, credentials, and motivations best fit the job the nonprofit has available. The prospective volunteer should complete an application that will be used to ensure a match of the right applicant to the right volunteer job.

Policy

Prospective volunteers must complete this Volunteer Application form (see Exhibit 8.2) as part of the process of determining the fit between the experience the volunteer is seeking and the qualifications needed for the volunteer work. Placement decisions are made by the volunteer coordinator, in consultation with the supervisors the volunteers will be reporting to, and the volunteer.

Volunteer Job Description

Rationale

A volunteer job description should be prepared for each type of volunteer job in the organization. This is a very useful tool for recruitment, placement, and supervision of volunteers. It provides the basis for the outreach program designed to find the right type of prospective volunteer. Clarity about what the job is and what is required to do it helps misunderstandings to be avoided.

Policy

Example Job Description

Nonprofit Organization Name, Contact Information

Mission of Nonprofit

Volunteer Job Description

Title: Fundraiser for Corporate Solicitations

| EXHIBIT 8.2 | VOLUNTEER APPLICATION |

Name: _____ Date: _____

Address: _____

Home phone: (__) _____ Business phone: (__) _____

Spouse's name: _____ Date of birth: _____

Parent name: _____ (for youth)

Name of someone in case of emergency: _____

Phone: (__) _____

Education degree and subject: _____

If a student, name school: _____

Paid work experience:

Have you done volunteer work at another nonprofit? If so, where?

List any special interests, skills, or hobbies:

What other languages beside English do you speak?

Do you have your own transportation? ☐ Yes ☐ No

What type of work would you like to do here?

Tell us why you want to volunteer at our nonprofit:

Please state the days and times available for volunteering:

How did you learn about our organization?

Please list three references. Include phone numbers and e-mail addresses where they can be reached:

Name	**Relationship**	**Phone**	**E-mail**
_____	_____	_____	_____
_____	_____	_____	_____
_____	_____	_____	_____

_____   _____

Signature   Date

General Description: Functions as a member of the Fundraising Committee of the Board of Directors. Helps plan and execute corporate solicitations.

Example of Duties:
- Attends fundraising committee meetings
- Helps identify corporate prospects
- Calls on corporations
- Prepares reports on corporate solicitations
- May train or supervise other volunteers who also make calls

Qualifications:
- Believes in the mission of this organization
- Willing to learn about the cause and the organization
- Good verbal skills
- Professional appearance
- Demonstrates interpersonal skills
- Has community contacts
- Previous fundraising experience desirable

Costs:
- Need to own transportation
- Provide for own gas, parking
- Ten hours per month on average available over a 1-year period.

VOLUNTEER RECORD KEEPING

Rationale

There are many benefits from maintaining volunteer personnel records:

- Conduct long-range planning for volunteer services
- Determine the cost value of volunteer services
- Determine volunteer trends
- Determine the number of active volunteers
- Document volunteer service for recognition

- Determine future needs for volunteers
- Collect specific demographic data
- Determine volunteer categories of service
- Maintain training records
- Assess future training needs
- Foster an expanding relationship with volunteers so they can support the cause in other ways, becoming effective advocates in the community
- Facilitate promotion of existing volunteers

Policy

Records will be kept on all volunteers and the services they render. All volunteers will have an individual personnel file, which will contain their application form, any other information obtained about them through the intake process, and a record of their services. Volunteers will have access to reviewing the contents of their own files on request. The personal information in the files will be kept confidential, as are personnel files on paid employees. The names of volunteers are made available for purposes of recognition of their services unless otherwise instructed by the volunteers in writing.

Statistics will be compiled on the services rendered both for each volunteer and the volunteer program itself.

VOLUNTEER RISK MANAGEMENT

Volunteers are a substantial asset of nonprofit organizations. However, there are potential liabilities associated with utilizing volunteers. The liability may be to the volunteer when something happens to them while volunteering for the organization. The volunteer, while working for the organization, may experience an event that creates a liability for the organization. Insurance can be obtained that may partially cover occurrences, but efforts should be made to reduce the likelihood of an incident that triggers liability concerns.

A nonprofit should evaluate the kinds of risk exposures within the organization. Steps that may reduce risks include insurance purchase, increased training, changing job design, or supervision and sharing the risk with others by contract. A knowledgeable insurance agent can respond with sound policy recommendations after the nonprofit has documented the types and numbers of volunteers, the jobs they perform, and completed a risk analysis. The insurance policies can then be designed to fit the situation rather than a generic version.[1]

Reference

1. The Nonprofit Risk Management Center, www.nonprofitrisk.com.

CHAPTER 9

Client and Client Services Policies

Nonprofits that provide direct services to clients may need policies concerning client rights and staff behavior with clients.

CLIENT CONFIDENTIALITY

Rationale

Except for access by authorized personnel, information about clients should be kept strictly confidential. Files should be kept secured. The HIPAA law covers issues of security of records for the health care industry, which affects many nonprofit organizations.

Policy

The Health Insurance Portability and Accountability Act of 1996 (HIPAA)

HIPAA is the acronym for the Health Insurance Portability and Accountability Act of 1996. The Centers for Medicare & Medicaid Services (CMS) is responsible for implementing various unrelated provisions of HIPAA, therefore HIPAA may mean different things to different people. Here's a directory of CMS's business activities with regard to HIPAA.

HIPAA Health Insurance Reform

Title I of the Health Insurance Portability and Accountability Act of 1996 (HIPAA) protects health insurance coverage for workers and their families when they change or lose their jobs. Visit this site to find out about pre-existing conditions and portability of health insurance coverage.

- HIPAA Insurance Reform

HIPAA Administrative Simplification

The Administrative Simplification provisions of the Health Insurance Portability and Accountability Act of 1996 (HIPAA, Title II) require the Department of Health and Human Services to establish national standards for electronic health care transactions and national identifiers for providers, health plans, and employers. It also addresses the security and privacy of health data. Adopting these standards will improve the efficiency and effectiveness of the nation's health care system by encouraging the widespread use of electronic data interchange in health care.

- HIPAA Administrative Simplification

Last Modified on Wednesday, October 16, 2002[1]

The Web site www.cms.hhs.gov/hippa/ provides extensive information as to any regulations regarding security of health care records.

Prior to release of any health care information, nonprofits should have clients sign that they have received and understand the confidentiality policies of the organization. The policy should allow for release of information as necessary to the client's insurance and other professionals who are part of the treatment plan.

USE OF PHYSICAL RESTRAINT

Rationale

Some nonprofits provide services to client who may need to be restrained. A policy covering the use of restraint is essential, and staff members should be familiar with the policy. Supervisors should ensure full compliance. The policy should clearly state the conditions when use of restraint is indicated and the means of restraint.

SUSPECTED ILLICIT ACTIVITY

Rationale

Nonprofits may wish to adopt a policy regarding reporting suspected illicit activity. The policy should identify the types of activity, reporting methods, and timing. The policy should commit to a prompt and objective investigation of any incident while safeguarding the rights of involved persons. Check state laws covering incidents involving minors.

Policy

Incident Report   The people this nonprofit serves shall not be subjected to bodily or verbal abuse, neglect, or any form of mistreatment by staff members, visitors, or others this nonprofit serves. Suspected illicit activity is to be reported promptly.

Definition: Illicit activity is any activity perpetrated against any person with whom this nonprofit is involved that is in violation of that person's rights, including, but not limited to, assault, rape or sexual assault, abuse, theft, or criminal conduct.

Any alleged violation shall be immediately reported to the supervisor on duty, who is responsible for initiating a thorough investigation and ensuring the details are recorded on an Incident Report form (see Exhibit 9.1). Failure to report any incident may be grounds for disciplinary action. The supervisor will maintain confidentiality as far as possible except for informing superiors and the executive director.

If the allegation is substantiated, the executive director shall be responsible for invoking appropriate discipline up to and including termination. This action will be recorded on a Corrective Action Notice form and will be placed in the staff member's personnel file. The executive director will report the incident to the appropriate authorities no later than the next working day.

EXHIBIT 9.1   INCIDENT REPORT

Type of Incident: _____

_____

Name of Person Reporting Incident:

_____

Street Address: _____

City/State/ZIP: _____

Phone Number: (___) _____

Birth Date: _____

Affiliation with Organization: _____

Witnesses (actual witnesses should sign own names):

_____   _____

_____   _____

_____   _____

_____   _____

Describe What Happened:

_____   _____

Signature of Reporting Person   Date

_____   _____

Signature of Supervisor Receiving Report   Date

_____

INFECTIOUS DISEASE POLICY

Rationale

Nonprofit organizations may wish to adopt a policy about infectious disease exposure at work. The policy can help individuals make proper judgments about when to stay home to avoid spreading disease and on how to protect coworkers from exposure to disease on the job.

Policy

Staff members should stay home during the contagious stages of infectious disease as instructed by their physician. Staff members must comply with safety and health regulations that limit transmission of disease.

AUDIOVISUAL CONSENT POLICY

Rationale

There are a number of reasons why a nonprofit would want to photograph or record people involved with the organization. Some of the reasons are publicity/fundraising/promotional purposes, staff training. Most people expect that if they attend a public event, they may have their picture taken as a part of the event coverage. However, if a person's image or voice is used for testimonials or in other ways to promote the organization, it is best to obtain a signed release from the person authorizing the audiovisual material to be available with his or her knowledge for specified use by the nonprofit.

FRATERNIZATION

Rationale

A policy prohibiting fraternization outside of the professional relationship between the staff person and the client helps to protect the clients and the organization. Some negative consequences from client/staff fraternization may be that clients may feel they will gain special privileges or may lose services as a result of the relationship with a staff person. The professional relationship may be abused intentionally or unintentionally.

The policy should state expectations regarding current and former clients and consequences for violating the policy.

REFERENCE

1. The Centers for Medicare & Medicaid Services, Washington, DC, www.cms.hhs.gov/hipaa/.

The Human Resource Cycle of Activities

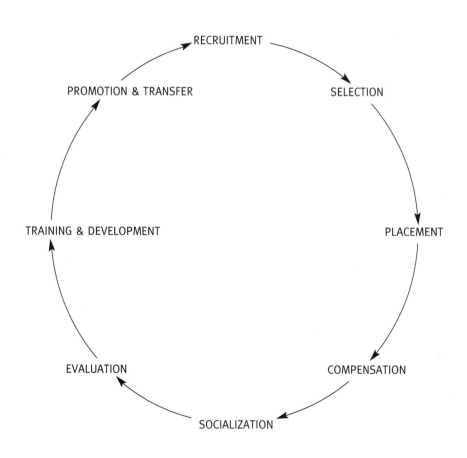

Action Steps for Attracting and Retaining Quality Personnel

1. To avoid over-compensation concerns, follow steps recommended for compliance with regulations for IRS Intermediate Sanctions. They are generally sound for all agencies.

2. Boards should be involved in setting compensation and then defend their decisions as needed. Other sector leaders and the media can interpret and support the need for fair and adequate compensation as appropriate and as the bedrock for successful mission accomplishment.

3. Accounting practices that allocate salary to the functions of the organizations can demonstrate that salaries are not overhead.

4. Funders, management assistance providers, other sector support organizations, plus the board and executive leadership of nonprofits should invest in the development of the human resource management systems.

5. Make the most of "cause" and "giving back" motivations, non-cash recognition and flexible work environments.

6. Know what rewards and conditions current employees value and what recruitment target markets value and take that into account when designing compensation plan.

7. Set compensation as a holistic package including wages, benefits and innovative compensation at levels needed to recruit and retain quality personnel.

8. Boards should actively monitor Executive Director satisfaction.

9. Boards can work in partnership with Executive Director.

10. Keep the composition of the Board up to date.

11. Both the Executive and the Board can invest in executive and staff development.

12. Executive Director acts assertively in obtaining adequate staff infrastructure and adequate compensation for all staff.

13. Board should discuss and prepare for succession planning.

Prepared by clb & associates.

Rate Yourself as a Volunteer Motivator

Instructions: Answer each of the following questions. Then rate your performance in each area on a 1–10 scale (10 best). Then mark the five areas you will work to improve in the next few weeks.

#	Question	Answer	Rating
1.	When was the last time you thanked a volunteer personally?		
2.	When was the last time you took a volunteer out for coffee or soda?		
3.	When was the last time you made a conscious effort to recognize your volunteer *by name?*		
4.	When did you last get together over lunch with your volunteer to talk informally?		
5.	When did you last ask a volunteer how they were or how they are enjoying their work?		
6.	When did you last update your volunteers on current developments in your agency?		
7.	When did you last have a party to honor your volunteers (or hold a special event in their honor)?		

(continues)

#	Question	Answer	Rating
8.	When was the last time you had your Executive Director/Board Chairman talk to your volunteers?		
9.	When was the last time you said, "We missed you." to a volunteer who has been out sick?		
10.	When was the last time you mentioned a volunteer in your newsletter or in the press?		
11.	When was the last time you gave a volunteer a *special* thank you such as: • a phone call; • flowers; • a personal letter?		
12.	When was the last time you held a meeting on a topic of special interest to your volunteers?		
13.	When was the last time you asked a volunteer for advice on an important decision (especially one effecting volunteers)?		
14.	When was the last time you honestly confronted a volunteer about a problem you're having with him/her?		
15.	When was the last time you had an informal review to find out what changes volunteers would like in your volunteer program?		
16.	When was the last time you asked your volunteers for suggestions about space allocations and other working conditions?		
17.	When was the last time you had your staff and volunteers together at a social event?		
18.	When was the last time you actually performed a volunteer job—just to get in touch with your volunteer's needs?		
19.	When was the last time you asked a volunteer for input about *their* job design (or new job design)?		
20.	When as the last time you inquired about the transportation needs of your volunteers?		
21.	When did you last have an exit interview with a volunteer and say thank you?		

Note: This worksheet is provided as an idea generator. The theory behind it is simple: The kind of recognition isn't as important as the fact that you systematically recognize your volunteers for their work. Also, recognition must be appropriate for the situation; the best recognition is still a sincere "thank you" when the job is well done.

Providing a Motivating Environment*

Providing a Motivational Environment and Being Fair . . . these 2 activities demand a linkage among at least 4 things:

- Job Descriptions
- Job Performance Standards
- Performance Evaluations, and
- Growth Plans

As leaders, one of the most important things we do is

- Elicit Peak Performance

When anyone is **not** doing a job well, there are 2 likely reasons:

1. Not capable
2. Not motivated

Simple test to find out which it is . . . ask this question:

"If the person's life depends on doing the work, can that individual do it?"

If the answer is "yes," the person is not motivated; If the answer is "no," the person is not capable of doing the work.

   If my life depends on flying assisted like a bird, I am in serious trouble. I simply cannot do it! All the screeching and arm-flapping in the world just isn't going to take me aloft!

But if I have to labor 18 hours a day for six weeks to get my work done, I probably *can* do that. May not want to. May not plan to, but I CAN.

It's a good idea to stay attentive to the REAL reasons for successes and for any failures to perform . . . Capability/Motivation!

If 2 things limit peak performance, then we probably have 2 ways to solve:

One is TRAINING

The other is MOTIVATION

You know a lot about training, so let's deal here with the motivation side of this issue . . . with 3 ideas for creating an environment where people can self-motivate.

1. **Linkage of:**
   - Job Descriptions
   - Job Performance Standards
   - Performance Evaluations, and
   - Growth Plans

Historically, motivation has been based on fear of punishment.

Less manual labor and more knowledge workers have resulted in some additional, better motivational methods.

One idea, Maslow's: Motivation is tied to NEEDS which causes DRIVES which results in MOTIVATION.

When a need is satisfied, it stops being a source of motivation.

A high degree of motivation requires:

   - A Continual Supply of Unsatisfied Needs

Physiological/Safety & Security/Social & Affiliation/Esteem & Recognition and Self-Actualization:

To cultivate achievement-driven motivation, we need an environment that values and emphasizes OUTPUT!

Knowing a lot in the abstract, and failing to apply that knowledge, isn't worth much.

Producing results is what matters! People who do this should be valued and highly esteemed!

To know where someone is in the motivational hierarchy, it is a good idea to observe their reaction to a pay raise. If the absolute sum of a raise in salary is important to the individual, then he or she operates at physiological or safety levels.

If, however, the motivation is how the raise stacks up to what others get, then esteem/recognition is a key operating concern and self-actualization is at play.

Sports/Playing Field/TEAMING
Be a COACH:

- Take no personal credit for the success of your team;
- Be demanding of the team;
- Be a player/coach; understand and care.

Money is a good motivator at lower levels of the hierarchy but, at higher levels, it motivates only **some** people only **some** of the time.

2. **Greatest Management Principle in the World:**
   Reward what you want done!★★

3. **TRM★★★**

TRM:	Task-relevant maturity (degree of achievement-orientation and readiness to take responsibility, as well as education, training, and experience) . . . specific to the task at hand.
TRM Low:	Precise, detailed instructions; Structured, task-oriented; Tell WHAT, WHEN, and HOW.
TRM Middle:	Communication, emotional support, and encouragement; mutual reasoning.
TRM High:	Managerial involvement is low; focus is on agreed-on objectives and monitoring.

Parental AND Managerial directions evolve from low TRM to high TRM.

IN SUMMARY:

3 of the many things valuable in eliciting peak performance:

- Linkage of:
  Job Descriptions
  Performance Standards
  Performance Evaluations, and Plans
- Rewarding What You Want Done
- Knowing the TRM of each individual; let that help guide growth

  AND, of course, a 4th, continuing to
- CATCH PEOPLE DOING THINGS RIGHT!

NOTES

★ Attribution for Providing a Motivating Environment, D. R. Linke, Ph.D., Domain, Inc., Lakewood, CO.

★★ Greatest Management in the World comes from a book of that title by Michael LeBoeuf. TRM is an idea from Andrew Grove in his book High Output Management.

★★★ High Output Management, Andrew Grove.

Administrative Simplification Under HIPAA: National Standards for Transactions, Security, and Privacy*

Overview

To improve the efficiency and effectiveness of the health care system, the Health Insurance Portability and Accountability Act (HIPAA) of 1996 included a series of "administrative simplification" provisions that required the Department of Health and Human Services (HHS) to adopt national standards for electronic health care transactions. By ensuring consistency throughout the industry, these national standards will make it easier for health plans, doctors, hospitals and other health care providers to process claims and other transactions electronically. The law also requires the adoption of security and privacy standards in order to protect personal health information. HHS is issuing the following major regulations:

- Electronic health care transactions (final rule issued);

- Health information privacy (final rule issued);

*Updated March 3, 2003

Information provided by Phoenix Health Systems (www.phoenixhealth.com) and HIPAAdvisory (www.hipaadvisory.com).

- Unique identifier for employers (final rule issued);
- Security requirements (final rule issued);
- Unique identifier for providers (proposed rule issued; final rule in development);
- Unique identifier for health plans (proposed rule in development); and
- Enforcement procedures (proposed rule in development).
- Although the HIPAA law also called for a unique health identifier for individuals, HHS and Congress have indefinitely postponed any effort to develop such a standard.

Under HIPAA, most health plans, health care clearinghouses and health care providers who engage in certain electronic transactions have two years from the time the final regulation takes effect to implement each set of final standards. More information about the HIPAA standards is available on HIPAAdvisory.com, HHS' Administrative Simplification Web site, and CMS' HIPAA Web site.

BACKGROUND

Today, health plans, hospitals, pharmacies, doctors and other health care entities use a wide array of systems to process and track health care bills and other information. Hospitals and doctor's offices treat patients with many different types of health insurance and must spend time and money ensuring that each claim contains the format, codes and other details required by each insurer. Similarly, health plans spend time and money to ensure their systems can handle transactions from various health care providers and clearinghouses.

Enacted in August 1996, HIPAA included a wide array of provisions designed to make health insurance more affordable and accessible. With support from health plans, hospitals and other health care businesses, Congress included provisions in HIPAA to require HHS to adopt national standards for certain electronic health care transactions, codes, identifiers, and security. HIPAA also set a three-year deadline for Congress to enact comprehensive privacy legislation to protect medical records and other personal health information. When Congress did not enact such legislation by August 1999, HIPAA required HHS to issue health privacy regulations.

Security and privacy standards can promote higher quality care by assuring consumers that their personal health information will be protected from inappropriate uses and disclosures.

In addition, uniform national standards will save billions of dollars each year for health care businesses by lowering the costs of developing and maintaining software and reducing the time and expense needed to handle health care transactions.

COVERED ENTITIES

In HIPAA, Congress required health plans, health care clearinghouses, and those health care providers who conduct certain financial and administrative transactions electronically (such as eligibility, referral authorizations, and claims) to comply with each set of final standards. Other businesses may voluntarily comply with the standards, but the law does not require them to do so.

To determine if a natural person, business, or government agency is a covered entity, the Centers for Medicare & Medicaid Services (CMS) provides a Covered Entity Decision Tree to guide you in determining whether you are a covered entity under the administrative simplification provisions of HIPAA. Many terms used in the tools are defined terms or have a special meaning. The definitions or special meanings will appear as footnotes on the relevant questions' pages to assist you.

COMPLIANCE SCHEDULE

In general, the law requires covered entities to come into compliance with each set of standards within two years following adoption, except for small health plans, which have three years to come into compliance. For the electronic transaction rule only, Congress in 2001 enacted legislation allowing a one-year extension for most covered entities provided that they submit a plan for achieving compliance. As a result, covered entities that qualify for the extension will have until Oct. 16, 2003 to meet the electronic transaction standards instead of the original Oct. 16, 2002 deadline. (Small health plans must still meet the Oct. 16, 2003 compliance date and are not eligible for an extension under the new law.) The legislative extension does not affect the compliance dates for the health information privacy rule, which remains April 14, 2003 for most covered entities (and April 14, 2004 for small health plans).

DEVELOPING STANDARDS

Under HIPAA, HHS must adopt recognized industry standards when appropriate. HHS works with industry standard-setting groups to identify and develop consensus standards for specific requirements. For each set of standards, HHS first develops proposed requirements to obtain public feedback. After analyzing public comments, HHS makes appropriate changes before issuing a final set of standards. The law also allows HHS to propose appropriate changes to the HIPAA regulations to ensure that the standards can be implemented effectively and be maintained over time to continue to meet industry needs.

ELECTRONIC TRANSACTION STANDARDS

In August 2000, HHS issued final electronic transaction standards to streamline the processing of health care claims, reduce the volume of paperwork and provide better service for providers, insurers and patients. HHS adopted modifications to some of those standards in final regulations published on Feb. 20, 2003. Overall, the new standards establish standard data content, codes and formats for submitting electronic claims and other administrative health care transactions. By promoting the greater use of electronic transactions and the elimination of inefficient paper forms, these standards are expected to provide a net savings to the health care industry of $29.9 billion over 10 years. All health care providers will be able to use the electronic format to bill for their services, and all health plans will be required to accept these standard electronic claims, referral authorizations and other transactions.

In December 2001, Congress adopted legislation that allows most covered entities to obtain a one-year extension to comply with the standards, from Oct. 16, 2002 to Oct. 16, 2003. To qualify for the extension, the covered entity must submit a plan for achieving compliance by the new deadline. (The legislation did not change the compliance date for small health plans, which remains Oct. 16, 2003.) HHS' Centers for Medicare & Medicaid Services (CMS) issued a model compliance plan that covered entities may use to obtain an extension.

Privacy Standards

In December 2000, HHS issued a final rule to protect the confidentiality of medical records and other personal health information. The rule limits the use and release of individually identifiable health information; gives patients the right to access their medical records; restricts most disclosure of health information to the minimum needed for the intended purpose; and establishes safeguards and restrictions regarding disclosure of records for certain public responsibilities, such as public health, research and law enforcement. Improper uses or disclosures under the rule are subject to criminal and civil sanctions prescribed in HIPAA.

After considering public comment on the final rule, HHS Secretary Tommy G. Thompson allowed it to take effect as scheduled, with compliance for most covered entities required by April 14, 2003. (Small health plans have an additional year.) In March 2002, HHS proposed specific changes to the privacy rule to ensure that it protects privacy without interfering with access to care or quality of care. After considering public comments, HHS issued a final set of modifications on Aug. 14, 2002. Detailed information about the privacy rule is available here on HIPAAdvisory.com and OCR's Web site.

Security Standards

In February 2003, HHS adopted final regulations for security standards to protect electronic health information systems from improper access or alteration. Under the security standards, covered entities must establish procedures and mechanisms to protect the confidentiality, integrity and availability of electronic protected health information. The rule requires covered entities to implement administrative, physical and technical safeguards to protect electronic protected health information in their care. The standards use many of the same terms and definitions as the privacy rule to make it easier for covered entities to comply. Most covered entities must comply with the security standards by April 21, 2005, while small health plans as defined by HIPAA will have an additional year to come into compliance.

Employer Identifier

In May 2002, HHS issued a final rule to standardize the identifying numbers assigned to employers in the health care industry by using the existing Employer Identification Number (EIN), which is assigned and maintained by the Internal Revenue Service. Businesses that pay wages to employees already have an EIN. Currently, health plans and providers may use different ID numbers for a single employer in their transactions, increasing the time and cost for routine activities such as health plan enrollments and health plan premium payments. Most covered entities must comply with the EIN standard by July 30, 2004. (Small health plans have an additional year to comply.)

Additional Standards

Led by CMS, HHS is currently developing other administrative simplification standards. HHS has published proposed regulations for national identifiers for health care providers—and is now reviewing public comments and preparing final regulations. HHS also is working to develop other proposed standards, including a national health plan identifier and additional electronic transaction standards. In addition, HHS is developing regulations related to enforcement of the adopted standards. The status of key standards required under HIPAA follows:

National Provider Identifier

In May 1998, HHS proposed standards to require hospitals, doctors, nursing homes, and other health care providers to obtain a unique identifier when filing electronic claims with public and private insurance programs. Providers would apply for an identifier once and keep it if they relocated or changed specialties. Currently, health care providers are assigned different ID numbers by each different private health plan, hospital, nursing home, and public program such as Medicare and Medicaid. These multiple ID numbers result in slower payments, increased costs and a lack of coordination.

NATIONAL HEALTH PLAN IDENTIFIER AND
OTHER HIPAA REGULATIONS

HHS is working to propose standards that would create a unique identifier for health plans, making it easier for health care providers to conduct transactions with different health plans. HHS is also working to develop additional transaction standards for attachments to electronic claims and for a doctor's first report of a workplace injury. In addition, HHS is developing a proposed rule on enforcement of the HIPAA requirements. As with other HIPAA regulations, HHS will first consider public comment on each proposed rule before issuing any final standards.

PERSONAL IDENTIFIER ON HOLD

Although HIPAA included a requirement for a unique personal health care identifier, HHS and Congress have put the development of such a standard on hold indefinitely. In 1998, HHS delayed any work on this standard until after comprehensive privacy protections were in place. Since 1999, Congress has adopted budget language to ensure no such standard is adopted without Congress' approval. HHS has no plans to develop such an identifier.

MODIFICATIONS TO STANDARDS

HIPAA mandates that the Secretary of Health and Human Services review the standards, and adopt modifications as appropriate, no more often than once every 12 months and in a manner that minimizes disruption and cost. The Secretary may not make any modifications during the 12 months following the effective date of a particular rule, unless the Secretary "determines that the modification is necessary in order to permit compliance."

SANCTIONS AND PENALTIES

Penalties established for noncompliance with HIPAA's requirements are:

- Personal liability: Individuals may be liable for up to 10 years in prison and $250,000 in fines for intentional misuse of protected health information

- Organizational liability: Healthcare organizations are liable for up to $25,000 in fines for each standard violated

Monetary Penalty	Imprisonment Penalty	HIPAA Offense
$100	N/A	Single violation of a provision
Up to $25,000	N/A	Multiple violations of an identical requirement or prohibition made during a calendar year
Up to $50,000	Up to one year	Wrongful disclosure of individually identifiable health information
Up to $100,00	Up to five years	Wrongful disclosure of individually identifiable health information committed under false pretenses
Up to $250,000	Up to 10 years	Wrongful disclosure of individually identifiable health information committed under false pretenses with intent to sell, transfer, or use for commercial advantage, personal gain, or malicious harm

- Accreditation: Accreditation organizations such as JCAHO are expected to require compliance in the future
- Federal Programs: Noncompliance is also expected to result in exclusion from federal programs such as Medicare

RELATIONSHIP TO STATE LAWS

HIPAA preempts state law except:

- where the state law is necessary to prevent fraud and abuse,
- to ensure state insurance or health plan regulation,
- to address controlled substances or for certain other purposes, and
- when state law is more stringent than HIPAA requirements.

IMPACT TO ORGANIZATIONS

Organizations need to consider a variety of issues when analyzing the impact of HIPAA on the organizations. These issues include:

- Purpose of HIPAA: In addition to ensuring patient privacy and information security, HIPAA is about improving the efficiency and cost-effectiveness of the healthcare system

- Limited resources, both in terms of dollars, staffing, and time—but which are necessary to implement these regulations

- Costs associated with implementation are currently difficult to assess; analysis of ROI is limited—but imperative—when analyzing various implementation strategies

- Convergence of e-health strategies and HIPAA objectives, which are clearly connected in the areas of standardization and technical security measures

- Constraining effects of legacy systems within industry, which add to cost of compliance as well as ongoing dependency on vendors

HIPAA will have a profound impact on overall healthcare industry electronic communications and transactions. Implementation of the information security and privacy features in HIPAA will pave the way for increasingly sophisticated e-health and other healthcare e-commerce and communications applications—as well as for new uses of evolving technologies, such as hand-held devices and wireless access. In order to realize these potential benefits—and to ensure that official compliance deadlines are met—healthcare organizations should begin immediately to assess their current information environment and develop strategies for HIPAA implementation.

Next Steps to Understanding HIPAA!

To learn more about HIPAA in plain English, read the HIPAA primer found at: http://www.hipaadvisory.com/regs/HIPAAprimer.htm.

Index

Terms with page numbers followed by "e" indicate an exhibit.

DATE DUE

APR 17 2013			
FEB 0 6 2017			
MAR 0 8 2017			

Demco, Inc. 38-293